THROUGH IMPERFECT LENS

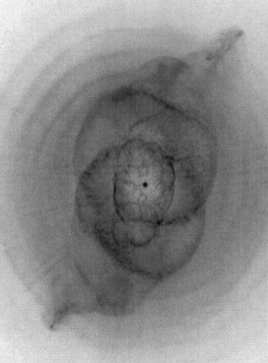

a true story of

Personal Growth and Relationship from a Psychospiritual Perspective

Elliot Talenfeld

THROUGH A STILL IMPERFECT LENS

*A True Story of Personal Growth and Relationship
from a Psychospiritual Perspective*

Printed in the United States of America

ISBN 978-0-9722498-3-6

Perach Press, Phoenix, AZ

To every heart so foolish
as to have no doubt, and
every mind so arrogant
as to have no faith;

* * *

and to everyone
who has ever tried
to change another person

Contents

BOOK TWO

SUPPLEMENTAL READING:
TWO *MIDRASHIM* (ALLEGORIES)

Author's Preface

From an early age, I have been a close observer of my moods, my interactions with others and the relationship between the two. Monitoring our internal, emotional status while simultaneously engaging with other people is a form of mental multi-tasking therapists call "process observation." If we actually interrupt the interaction to discuss the interpersonal dynamics, that is called "process commentary." This book is a partial record of my lifetime of process observation and commentary.

To this day, I continue to put journaling pen to yellow pad (or mouse to cursor) as a way of wrestling with just what is going on between me and those with whom I am emotionally engaged. Indeed, my fascination with process finally called me, at the mature age of 58, to train for a second career, as a counselor.

But beyond the ever dwindling cadre of talk-therapists, the art of process observation and commentary is not professional *per se.* Freud and his progeny may have articulated the concept, but lay human beings have been paying attention to their emotions and, perhaps less frequently, talking about them, probably since Cain slew Abel. Even in psychotherapy, it is said that the professional relationship has run its course once the patient/client has learned to do his own process observation as a matter of acquired self-awareness and interpersonal self-discipline.

Now in my first career, as an attorney, it was considered unlawyerlike to even *have* emotions much less comment upon them. In large law firms, where billable time is zealously guarded, touchy-feely types like me are considered "high maintenance." My narrative will illustrate just what can happen when a misfit, counselor-in-waiting smuggles contraband process commentary into the mental-argumentative juggernaut.

But taking lawyers and therapists out of the mix, most people probably do pay more attention to their material (five-sensory) balance sheet than their emotional (*psychosensory*) one—at least until someone accuses them of being "in need of professional help." Yet even our subliminal emotional stirrings no less impact our subjective quality of life (and ultimately, our behavior). So in the psychological discussion that accompanies my narrative, I will be using the undifferentiated term "sensation" to encompass our subtler and ever-fluctuating emotional field, right along with the more obvious stream of physical data pouring in through the five senses.

I will lump those physical and emotional components together precisely to distinguish the holistic but still individual experience from its relational consequences. So "sensation" will address our moment to moment, sensory-*cum*-emotional status, whether conscious or preconscious, positive or negative, and regardless of what we may be doing or with whom we may be doing it. "Relation" will capture the interpersonal repercussions of our individual experience (depending, to be sure, on what we *do* with it).

And of course the "what" and the "with whom" certainly influence our psychosensory status, creating a constant feedback loop between sensation and relation. Just how that works, how our relationships affect our emotions and vice-versa, is what this book is all about. (As a sneak preview, my hypothesis is that our significant relationships serve as both the laboratory and the spiritual *catalyst* for our personal growth and emotional healing.)

Now my dear wife, whose bent is more practical than hypothetical, has occasionally begrudged me the pedantic lengths to which I can go, e.g., in the preceding three paragraphs. She points out that if this book is to be read, it must be narrative, not treatise (hence the subtitle, "a true *story* of personal growth and relationship"). And that works for me (theoretically), since I believe anything truly taught or learned must first, in some way, have been personalized.

I can also happily report that our relational story (a second marital one for both of us) is alive and kicking. So should she happen to email me, say in the next five minutes, she is unlikely to inquire, point blank, whether I am still working on this dense and unnecessary preface. She will ask, instead, whether I have taken the clothes to the cleaners.

Years of process observation have taught me that in our household at least, "clothes to cleaners" is a subset of "billable time." So when she broaches this sensitive subject again, however obliquely, it will behoove me (*and* the relationship) to *think* before I respond. After which, instead of raising a defensive fuss, I will assure her that the dirty clothes are quickly rising to the top of my busy agenda (a true statement, however beside the point). For no good purpose would be served, in this hypothetical, by pointing out that a story about process observation and commentary necessarily entails a fair amount of interpretive material, in anticipation of which this brief philosophical framework is entirely called for.[i]

In a related vein, let me say a word about the narrowly circumscribed professional process in which mental health practitioners engage. In complete contrast to their clients/patients, from whom they work diligently to elicit both affect and authenticity, therapists deliberately *suppress* any emotional reaction they themselves may be having to what the client is presenting. (In clinical parlance, such emotion on the therapist's part is called "countertransference.") For while nonprofessional process observers are under no such constraint, therapists are admonished to attend to but *not get mixed up in* the client's emotional or relational life.[ii]

But in *The Road Less Traveled,* a book that greatly influenced me, the late M. Scott Peck suggested that "any genuinely loving relationship is one of *mutual psychothera-*

---

[i] For a further academic treatment of the epistemology and interplay between sensation and relation, see the two Supplemental Readings at the end of the book. (And know that it was *she* who made me move them all the way back there.)

[ii] There is an important difference between suppression and *repression*, the elaboration of which would truly make this a treatise. Suffice it to say that the therapist certainly takes note of his internal reactions to the client (which can be clinically instructive), but does not share or act upon them unless there is some compelling clinical reason to do so.

py." If so, the role and proper management of countertransference is something we must all come to grips with. For it is inevitable, indeed *desirable* that we become emotionally engaged in our loved-one's process (in which we, unlike the therapist, have a personal and ongoing stake.)[iii]

And therein lies the "catch 22" of our love relationships. For the therapy gets much dicier once it becomes a two-way street, when the spouse-therapist is called not to censor his emotions but to voice them. Our emotional give and take, after all, is what tends to bring us to the therapist or marriage counselor in the first place. In short, it is much harder to *have* a relationship than to counsel one.

So I am not suggesting that every feuding couple sit right down and practice mutual therapy on each other, especially if drugs or alcohol, serious mental illness or any history of violence are involved. Sometimes, we certainly *do* need professional help. That said, the experiences I will be relating in this book have convinced me that Peck's dictum is fundamentally sound. And that objectivity and emotionality, if strange bedfellows, are not mutually exclusive.

Indeed, I believe it is possible for reasonably healthy couples who love each other to move well beyond ordinary defensive banter and learn to explore their own and each other's psychodynamics—even and precisely when they are manifesting in the form of relational conflict. For the ultimate goal of our lay process observation, it seems to me, is the mature realization that our respective inner (*intra*-per-

[iii] Some of my dialogue with Peck about the implications of "mutual therapy" is related in Chapters 25-29.

sonal) conflicts have, in fact, been coming at each other's expense; and more importantly, that they need not continue, all our relational lives, to do so.

I also realize as I write this that it will be fairly easy for anyone reading this book to cite my own relational experience as the best evidence to the contrary. Reasonable minds may differ on that point, but I see my self-experimental cup as at least half full; and continue to believe that the committed relationship affords the best portal through which to uncover and address those individual psychodynamics that truly matter. (For a more detailed discussion of this, see Chapters 9-11.)

I am a proud and AARP card-carrying baby boomer. As such, I have participated in my share of the sometimes undisciplined interpersonal experimentation for which our generation is both famous and notorious. That experience will be front and center of my narrative (and the object of some older-but-wiser criticism). Nevertheless, as I write of these experiences today, I still marvel at our bold idealism and feel a twinge of sadness that our enthusiasm for process does not seem to have been passed down to the younger generations.

In my coursework to become a counselor, I was struck by the proliferation of books and articles linking psychology and spirituality. Indeed, while interning at an agency called the Center for Life Enrichment, I wrote an article observing that modern psychology now ventures right up to and sometimes beyond the line that used to demarcate the one from the other:

What we call "behavioral health" is more remedial than proactive. It attempts to relieve clinical dysfunction, by diagnosing and treating emotional disorders. The Diagnostic and Statistical manual (D.S.M.), used by virtually all mental health practitioners, is thus a categorical way of looking at things. The patient either has or does not have a particular disorder, depending on the number, combination and duration of the presenting symptoms.

But some have argued that mental health is better conceptualized as a continuum of personal growth, ranging from psychosis, at one end, to the person's highest psychological potential, at the other. Indeed, the phrase "positive psychology" has been coined to capture this idea. With a focus on our potential rather than our pathology, positive psychology promotes personal growth for the already well adjusted.

In this book, I presume to take the discussion a step farther, from "positive-psychology" to the full-on integration of psychology and spirituality. So just a brief further word about what I have in mind when I use yet another hybrid term, "psychospiritual."

Early in my narrative, it will be evident that my worldview is heavily colored by my Jewish upbringing and education. And I think it fair to say that both Judaism's fundamentally communal orientation and its emphasis on *tikun olam* -- repair of the world" (rather than personal salvation) have tended to make us the behaviorists of the world's religions. Indeed, it may be our relative de-emphasis of individual transcendental experience that drove me and so many of my fellow Jewish baby boomers into the vanguard of New-Age and eastern religious movements, as will be described below.

Nevertheless, there has always been a more mystical strain of Judaism, and I personally look to the Hebrew word *"kavana"* for my here-and-now connection to it. *"Kavana"* means inner aim, or spiritual intent. As Jews begin to pray, we are adjured to take aim at a threshold state of humility and sincerity that will empower our prayer. *"Adonai, s'fatai tiftach,"* we begin, which I read "Lord, open up my *heart,* so that I may experience and make good use of this personal time with You."

We could think of this as *"kavana beyn adam leMakom* -- spiritual intent as between us and God." But we can also think of *kavana* along the interpersonal dimension (*"beyn adam lechevro* -- between us and our fellow human beings"). In that mode, which I am calling the *relational,* our spirituality *goes forth,* from the religious/ceremonial into the behavioral/interactive. And I believe this latter, person-to-person type of *kavana* is what sanctifies our relationships and *empowers tikun olam.*

But this implies more than just ethical behavior, however scrupulous. For as white bread offers calories but scant nutrition, we can be morally irreproachable without giving (or receiving) much spiritual nourishment. So for me as a Jew, the concept of horizontal (interpersonal) *kavana* gears the abstract "spiritual" down into the more humanly accessible realm I am calling the psychospiritual (and from there, to the even more manifest ethical/behavioral).

This idea is explored in Chapter 8, the title of which is

"Energy," and the Jewish reader is invited to substitute *"kavana,"* as interpreted above, for that chapter title. The psychospiritual implication of both terms, as I am using them, is that we owe it—at least to those we claim to love—to become more emotionally self-aware. This means taking responsibility not just for our overt behavior but for the psychosensory effect our very *presence* is having on those within our emotional/energetic sphere.

Since my story also involves gurus, psychic healers and trance mediums, I should draw a distinction here between the "psychic" (in the E.S.P. or paranormal sense) and what I am calling the psychospiritual. I believe that psychic or paranormal phenomena, however intriguing, are (like emotion) just a further extension of our better understood five senses. However "extra," they remain "sensory," i.e., not spiritual *per se.*[iv]

So when I use the prefix "psycho," in "psychosensory" and "psychospiritual," I have in mind the individual-emotional, in the first instance, and what I hold to be the more spiritual-relational, in the second. For I believe it is in relationship that we find and raise up those scattered *kabbalistic* sparks; that the psychological is the linchpin (and our conduit) between the material world and the spiritual; and that our love for those we hold most dear (when we allow ourselves to fully feel and express it) is the still imperfect lens through which we glimpse the face of God.

[iv] Taking a break from editing this preface, I turned on the radio just as Diane Rehm was interviewing pianist Byron Janis. Coincidently (or paranormally), he was talking about his new book, *Chopin and Beyond: My Extraordinary Life in Music **and the Paranormal***. Mr. Janis was suggesting that a better term for "paranormal" is "the unknown normal," or "the normal we haven't yet quite been able to figure out."

I do though see a connection between our emotions and the specific form of E.S.P. we call intuition. I believe that emotion is *nascent* intuition, which, in order to blossom as such, must be buffered from the corrupting influence of ego. What the conventional wisdom overlooks is that maintaining objectivity, once the emotional dust has been kicked up, is more a personal/spiritual than a clinical/professional challenge. It is about keeping the *ego,* not the emotions, in check.[v]

As discussed in Chapters 12 and 26, I see ego as the mother of all defensiveness. When a conflict erupts, it circles like a vulture, hoping to subvert the parties' will to communicate. And when ego penetrates our emotional field, defensiveness is the behavioral product. Defensiveness is our neurotic stasis, energized by projection and then commandeered by ego. It is emotion "gone bad."

Our very reactivity to someone else's communication thus alerts us that objectivity is, to that extent, *at risk.* But the interaction may yet prove a blessing, depending on what happens next. If we hand ego the reins, our relational work-in-process degenerates into defensiveness, sabotaging the communication. But if ego can be contained, emotion will *ripen*—into the same intuition on which the therapist ultimately relies.

I therefore recommend we pay attention to ego as part and parcel of our process observation. As therapists must bracket (contain) their own emotions, in service of their clients, husbands and wives must learn to bracket their

[v] Of course, I am using "ego" here in the self-important, colloquial sense, not the Freudian.

egos, for the love of each other and in service of the relationship.

A final word about the nature of this writing. Memoirs are personal by definition, and this one exposes my most intimate and, speaking of ego, often unflattering interactions. Indeed, as the living-out and writing-up of these encounters has worn on (and on), maintaining my professional life and credibility has been a challenge (and as for the credibility part, not terribly successful).

But perhaps the length of time it has taken to complete this project will prove one more blessing in disguise. For now in semi-retirement and with my children grown, I feel freer to make these self-disclosures without resort to a pseudonym. Nevertheless, out of respect for those who might prefer to remain anonymous, I have changed everyone *else's* names and the locales of the events described. I have also lightly edited the correspondence, for clarity, and added a metaphor or two to the dialogue, for color.

That said, every incident and every conversation reported in this book actually did happen. *("EMES -- for real!")*

"Harofey lishvurey lev umechabeysh l'atzvotam -- May our broken hearts be mended and all our wounds bound up."

BOOK ONE

*"Any genuinely loving relationship
is one of mutual psychotherapy."*

M. Scott Peck, *The Road Less Traveled*

PROLOGUE

The phone rang. It was Mitch. Diane took the call in the kitchen. I stayed in the living room but could hear her side of the conversation.

He was upset about something, and my wife was soothing him. More. She was loving him over the phone. I don't mean "phone-sex." It was just obvious how much she truly cared for him.

When she returned to the living room I was upset but not angry. "Look," I said to her, "we've both agonized over this situation with Mitch. I've even gone so far as to ask Sarah whether the two of you have done the deed. She said, 'not yet,' but suggested I hire a private detective. The fact is, I don't need a detective to interpret what I just heard. You *love* this guy. I'm not going to call that 'wrong' or try to put a stop to it. But why don't we just call this heart a heart?"

"Sarah was wrong," Diane responded. "We have gone all the way. I don't want to hurt you any further. I guess we should get a divorce."

I went to see a divorce lawyer. Diane called and made an appointment with one. Then she disappeared.

She didn't seem herself when she left the house that evening. But who was I, under the circumstances, to be giving her a pep talk?

3

When her mother called the next day, I told her Diane had driven off the night before and hadn't returned. "Well, did you go *after* her?" she demanded. "No" was my only reply.

I was numb. There was nothing to do but wait. For the first time in our married life, I was the emotional spectator Diane had always seemed.

A day and a half passed before I bothered to call Sarah. She worried about a car wreck. "Have you checked the hospitals?" she asked. Once again, "No" was all I could muster.

"I have to put the phone down," Sarah said. A few moments later, she came back and announced that Diane was "out of harm's way." "I don't know what they *mean* by that," she continued, as if questioning her own guidance. "I think she's at your old house in Normal; please call a neighbor there and have them check."

I had gotten no answer at the Normal house the day before. Somehow, it hadn't occurred to me to phone the neighbors. They soon confirmed Diane's car was parked out front. "All the lights are on, but she doesn't answer," they reported. "What do you want us to do?"

"Go in," I replied.

It was 45 minutes before they called me back. The boys were asleep, and I'd been pacing around, imagining the most likely scenarios . . . and how I would explain them to our children.

"There's been a suicide attempt," the neighbor intoned. "The paramedics are here."

"Is she conscious?" I asked.

"Yes."

"Is she coherent?"

"Somewhat. She's lost a lot of blood. We're going to ride with her in the ambulance; we'll call you from the hospital."

It was a two-hour drive from my location to the hospital in Normal. I thought about racing over there, but then I'd be incommunicado. And under the circumstances, I didn't want to leave the kids alone.

The neighbors in Normal called back and put the emergency room doctor on briefly. "We're trying to stabilize her," he said. "I've got to get back in there. I'll call you again as soon as I can."

I phoned my sister in Cleveland. The first plane would get her here around midnight. I told her I'd leave the door unlocked and write a note for the kids, in case they woke up before she got there.

But I was still there when my sister arrived. The doctor had called back to say they were going to air-evac Diane to Northwestern Memorial, where a surgeon would be standing by. She had gotten to within a millimeter of the jugular vein. Until the surgery, it would be impossible to know whether she had done permanent damage. But it was now at least safe to transport her.

I was there when the helicopter landed. Diane had a gaping wound in her neck. She spoke in the voice of a little girl who was the center of attention. She was smiling, almost bubbly.

"I *realized* something," she told me excitedly before they wheeled her into surgery. "After talking to the lawyer,

I knew I couldn't go through with the divorce. You've always been there for me . . . and it's you I want by me now."

PART ONE

SENSATION

1

Call JEFLER

Even in English, "O Lord our God and God of our fathers" was a mouthful for a 9-year-old. So, feeling certain we knew each other well enough to dispense with such formality, I decided to give God a nickname, something we'd keep between the two of us. (And in an emergency, God forbid, He would also know right away that it was me.)

Our covenant in those days was just that personal and straightforward, simple enough for a child to understand. My job was to behave; His, to make sure only good things happened to my family and me.

That being the whole point, it occurred to me to use the initial letters of all our first names to form an acronym. With two parents and three siblings, I had four consonants and two EEs to work with.

And so, like an invisible med-alert bracelet, I bound Him for a sign around our wrists:

> JEFLER IS OUR GOD.
> IN EMERGENCY,
> CALL JEFLER.

Our synagogue, B'nai Israel, was a grand and mysterious place that went well with my childish theology. Just inside the Negley Avenue entrance, a tunnel-like corridor wound steeply around the sanctuary's perimeter. Its curved slope connoted an ascending pilgrimage, especially for those with little or tired old legs.

At the summit, one came into a cavernous hall with a high, domed ceiling. Chandeliers in the shape of giant Stars of David twinkled brightly. Down a long center aisle, the rich mahogany Ark, resplendent with gold-painted lions, rose up 25 feet from the dais. And hidden behind its sliding wooden doors, then a sheer white curtain, were the sacred Torah scrolls, each ornately garbed and crowned.[1]

Once, around the time JEFLER got His name, I sneaked into the darkened sanctuary. It was a spooky scene, the only light being the red *Ner Tamid* (Eternal Light) that hung above the Ark. Standing in that awesome space, I wondered what would happen were I to steal a bit farther . . . right up into the Ark itself! Might I then feel like one of God's own Torah scrolls, holy and beloved?

On Saturday mornings, the choir sang from a loft so high up it evoked an angelic presence. They accompanied the Cantor,[2] who pled our case with high notes so vigorous they turned his whole face red. Yet when the liturgical mood shifted, he could also beseech God in a sacred falsetto whisper.

We rose to our feet when the Ark was finally opened. As

[1] Each Torah scroll contains the first five books of the Bible, handwritten on parchment.

[2] In traditional congregations, the cantor leads the worship service, chanting the prayers, in Hebrew.

the Cantor reached in to remove one of the Torahs, its silver crown and breastplate jangled in anticipation of the excursion down into the hubbub of the congregation. *"Ki mitziyon teytzey Torah,"* sang the choir -- "Out of Zion shall go forth the Law." The Cantor then led a procession around the sanctuary, pausing for those who wished to kiss the Torah . . . and singing majestically all the while.

His voice was my Pied Piper. When I was old enough to take my place in the celestial choir loft, the first thing I had to learn was how to funnel so large an exuberance into just the small sound I was trying to emit. Sometimes, it was all I could do to mouth the words.

Singing was thus my first love, but also the source of my earliest disillusionment. For all too soon it was clear that my vocal reach was exceeding my grasp. The solos were going to other members of the youth choir. Then, as my Bar Mitzvah approached, my voice began cracking, unpredictably.

God smiled on me that day, and I made it through in rare form. It was as though I'd been granted a boon, one opportunity to sing decently and uninhibitedly before the ax fell. Thereafter, my adolescent vocal "gap" continued to widen, to the point I simply couldn't produce anything remotely resembling a well-placed tone.

In high school, my musicianship (if not my singing) endeared me to our choir director, a formidable spinster who brooked no nonsense. Out of the blue one day, as though JEFLER Himself had put the word in, she anointed me her student-conductor. Soon thereafter, she sent me to take a musical aptitude test at the local conservatory.

My scores confirmed a good facility for pitch, rhythm

and such. But the fine print cautioned that first and foremost, an aspiring musician must show distinct vocal or instrumental promise. And someone had placed three asterisks beside that admonition, as if I might have missed it.

Meanwhile, in the B'nai B'rith Youth Organization, I was learning to make rousing speeches that in time, would get me elected president of a multi-state district. My picture appeared in the local *Jewish Chronicle,* making me a veritable poster child for what an active Jewish teenager should be.

But for all this outward display of Jewish identity and conviction, my memory of these pre-adolescent and teenage years includes, just under the behavioral surface, a budding spiritual malaise. For as the growth spurt within my Adam's apple had disrupted my vocal registers, some slower, cerebral process was now taking aim at my religiosity. Indeed, within just a few years of the pinnacle that was my Bar Mitzvah, a chasm had opened up between my nascent, worldly sensibilities and the ceremony that had once so moved me.

Judaism, to be sure, was no less rich in religious symbolism and ethical substance. But my own inner shine, what our sacred objects merely reflect back to us, seemed to have tarnished. A phrase from the Sabbath prayer book comes to mind: *"Chadeysh yameynu kekedem* -- Renew our days as of old."

Some modicum of resistance to religious doctrine or observance is probably part of normal development, calling us from our bright-eyed but ineffectual childhood into a more capable if less impressionable adulthood. But I believe my growing skepticism was of a more virulent, Ashkenazi strain, to which Jewish teens of my generation had virtually no resistance. For in the sixties, we were still reeling from the shock of the Holocaust. Is it surprising, at such a low point in our long history, that personal communion with God (which seemed not to have availed the six million) should have taken a back seat to a more sectarian, less overtly spiritual religious life?

The Zionists championed our physical survival, but American Jews were not threatened in that immediate, corporeal way. What my elders feared was the further decimation of our ranks by assimilation into the wider (secular) American culture. The litmus test for an upstanding Jew thus came to be a deferred one—would his *grandchildren* grow up to "identify Jewishly" (whatever that might mean by then)? Or would our more gradual and voluntary disappearance no less hand Hitler his final (if posthumous) solution?

Of course, the Orthodox measure of Jewish living remained the dutiful, i.e., unquestioning performance of *mitzvot* (religious commandments). But for the less devout majority, our sectarian identity subsisted on an often lackluster showing-up for holidays and lifecycle events (where you could at least always count on a good meal). In that environment, Jewish communal leadership seemed to fall to those who could articulate a "Jewish point of view" on the subject at hand, with poise, verbal clarity and mental conviction. Like good lawyers, in short. But neither the message nor the modeling bespoke any kind of direct, personal or life-influencing relationship . . . *with God*.

In my current late-middle adulthood, I must admit that placing such modifiers ("direct, personal, or life-influencing") next to the abstraction many of us have come to call "God" gives me some pause, sounding almost "un-Jewish."

But this, I think, makes my very point. Going back just a handful of generations (and from there, all the way back to Abraham), we Jews have had, at the very center of our identities, a distinctly personal (if uniquely collective) relationship with *Hashem Eloheynu,* the Lord our God. I believe our more recent resort to Jewish culture and/or "peoplehood" as a *raison d'etre,* i.e., uninformed by any immanent deistic sensibility, has left us emancipated, but spiritually bereft.

How a post-Holocaust Jew recaptures (or reframes) a relationship with God, assuming he still wants one, is no small dilemma. I can only say that during my formative years, my religious mentors had little to offer in this regard. Indeed, they seemed not really to want the job. "Fine," it was as if they were saying. "How very bright of you to be skeptical. We hereby pass the torch of Jewish communal leadership on to *your* clever generation."

Nevertheless, from my still formative perch half a century later, I can see that well before this problem had even gotten my attention, some latent yearning, for chosen-*personhood,* was already stirring in that little boy gazing up in awe at the Holy Ark. And like some hidden *kabbalistic* thread reaching back through the generations, setting the stage for the quite confusing, sometimes torturous but ever soul-searching saga he would live to report below.

2

Formal Studies

Whatever my spiritual ambivalence in those high school years, I continued my religious education at Pittsburgh's College of Jewish Studies. In actuality, this was just an extension of Hebrew or Sunday school for the handful of us willing to study on beyond bar or bat mitzvah. But something I said or wrote there apparently caught the eye of the dean of the institution, on whose nomination I was unexpectedly offered a scholarship for a year of college study— in Israel!

At that time, neither our family nor our synagogue were what anyone would call "Zionist." No one we knew had ever visited Israel (much less emigrated there). But in the face of this adventuresome opportunity, commuting to one of our local colleges, as my sister and brother had done, quickly lost all luster. So in the summer of 1965, my parents drove me to New York City, where I boarded the s.s. Zion, bound for Haifa.

What a foreign and third-worldly place Israel seemed to me in those still early days of its statehood. On one hand, it did feel like a homecoming, in the sense that everybody (except of course for the Arabs) felt like family. If you stepped off the curb before the light changed, some "bubbie" you'd never met (but always known) would pipe up: "Such an important *person,* and in a *big hurry! So what* if his poor mother should cry her eyes out when she hears he's been *hit by a bus!"* And it was both novel and empowering for me to *see* Jewish bus drivers, police and garbage collectors, all working with more (not less) self-respect for the very pedestrian practicality and nation-building relevancy of their labor.

That said, nothing about the land itself felt familiar to me. I was moved by the biblical and historical significance of the holy sites we visited (as much as a 17- year-old tends to be moved by such things). But I did not experience that unique geographic locus of Jewish spirituality *cum* nation-hood so poetically evoked in *Hatikva.* I cannot say I felt a terrestrial "welcome-home," welling up from the very real estate.

Still, my year in Israel left me with an enduring con-nection to the country, such that I still scan each day's headlines for developments there, particularly on the peace front. (And pray, as my ancestors have done for two mil-lennia, for the welfare of Jerusalem.)

While I was away in Israel, my father took a job in Chicago, so on my return, the Windy City and Loyola Uni-versity became my new home. Though my declared major at Loyola was political science, I nevertheless inflicted my-self on the school's *A Cappella* Choir and even signed up for a formal voice class. But after a willful semester of vo-cal calisthenics, I ended up with a "C" in the course (not the tenor high-C to which I so aspired). When I protested that I had diligently done everything the instructor had asked of me, his response was, "Yes, I know; but *you* didn't improve."

The silver lining was that on the very first day of that otherwise futile class, I met Diane. Having been called upon to introduce myself vocally to the group, I had just begun crooning "Jerusalem of Gold" when she entered the room. "You had me on 'Jerusalem,'" she would later confide.

And "having her" soon became my extracurricular obsession. For my sexual urge (like my vocal one) was also going unrequited. But Diane was now flashing the hottest contralto ever to show an interest in my fervid if underachieving vibrato.

The time will come for me to own up to the karma of my youthful priorities. Suffice it for now to say that we dated all through college, by which time our duets had long proved greater than the sum of my solo part. And we married soon after graduation.

I had also signed up for a cantorial workshop offered by a local branch of the Hebrew Union College. The class met for three hours each Tuesday night, at the synagogue of the cantor-instructor. How strange to see the elaborate prayer modes written out note for note, with English transliteration. Hooked on this immediately, I had little difficulty mastering the material from a musical or linguistic standpoint.

And being just as gifted a singer as a brand new congregation could afford actually made me the perfect part-time cantor when Temple *Adat Elohim* opened its door. But as the Temple's coffers began to swell, the karma encrypted on my vocal cords proved immune to perseverance. So when they could afford better, my vocation had little choice but to give way to my eventual career.

Law school proved exhilarating, particularly in comparison to my undergraduate course work in political science. Here at last was a subject matter that truly mattered. The fate of the disputants turned on how we reconciled their opposing positions in light of society's larger values and competing social agendas.

I found this a most satisfying integration of abstract reasoning and day-to-day practicality. Unlike most of my classmates, who seemed to bear the curriculum as a kind of academic hazing on their way to professional standing and a decent livelihood, I actually enjoyed the law. For me, it was the transition to earning a living that would pose the greater challenge.

This was complicated by the fact that halfway through law school, I began exploring spiritual life in formats totally alien to my Jewish upbringing. It all started when one of the lawyers at the firm where I was doing a summer internship invited me along to his regular, Sunday morning yoga lesson. Ironically enough, the teacher was a religiously observant Jewish woman who happened to have her own hatha-yoga studio!

On the surface, hatha-yoga is a physical discipline consisting of a series of postures, held with a high degree of concentration. But almost from the start of that class, I sensed that more than my spine was flexing and relaxing. With each long, measured breath, I could feel my cluttered *psyche* unlimbering. An hour and a half later, I was in such a wonderfully calm but alert state that I promptly signed up for my own weekly yoga lessons.

My third year of law school proved a welcome respite from the competitiveness of the first two years. On the strength of my performance as a summer intern, the firm had guaranteed me a position a full year ahead of graduation. I thus was spared the rigors of job hunting with which my classmates were contending. The curriculum itself was less demanding, and with my immediate future secure, maintaining a high class ranking also lost its urgency.

It was during this happy time that I picked up a copy of *Autobiography of a Yogi,* by Parmahansa Yogananda. In the life story of this inspired swami, I found an exotic yet vaguely familiar approach to God and religion. Had I not known such reverence myself, years before? Yogananda's writing reminded me of the little boy who had wanted to be a Torah scroll; and made me wonder what had ever become of that precocious child's naive but endearing thrust for holiness.

I thus emerged from law school with all the qualifications for budding leadership in the Jewish community. I had the birthright, the education, a Jewish wife and one of the preferred professional pedigrees, to boot. I had even taken a summer-school class with famed Rabbi Mordecai Kaplan and could expound upon his theory of God as "the Power that makes for Salvation" (even if I couldn't *apply* it in any personally useful way).

But that was to become the fly in my spiritual ointment. For what I hadn't learned from my Judaic curriculum, communal activism or that year in Israel was how to establish a sense of *connection* . . . with *Hashem Eloheynu.*

Then unexpectedly, some ancient childish impetus began flickering again, like a personal *Ner Tamid.* And for the moment at least, Swami Yogananda was the unlikely custodian of its sacerdotal flame.

3

Signs and Wonders

Yogananda stressed that it was possible to know God experientially, not just metaphorically. I had seen this in tracts handed out by missionaries of various stripe (which I'd dismissed as so much self-delusion on their part). Perhaps what was different about Yogananda's message was that he was telling the story of his own life, not threatening me with eternal damnation. In all events, my circumstances now allowed me the time and energy for some spiritual experimentation.

One day, after an hour or so of yoga postures and deep breathing, I felt particularly alert and focused. "Why not give it a try?" I asked myself. "Give what a try?" I answered. "You know, the talking to *God* thing."

Since no one was looking, I allowed myself, just barely, to continue along these lines. I did some more deep breathing and found my attention gathered at the spot between the eyebrows sometimes called the "third eye." I fancied myself putting out a signal-beam to God's 1-800 number.

"Okay, I'm here. I'm skeptical. (In fact if ever asked, I'll probably deny we *had* this conversation.) But if You're there and willing to make contact, I'd welcome some response."

Yogananda, I remembered, had a guru to help him make the divine connection. Indeed, he had seen the face of his spiritual teacher in meditation before meeting him in the flesh. Willing to settle for such a sign, I began conjuring up visages of current-day holy people whose names I'd seen on placards or in books.

"What if asking for this kind of thing (or even 'being open to it') means I've already *half lost my mind?"* I panicked. "Oh, give it a rest," some more adventuresome part of me prodded. "You'll either get some kind of response or you won't." So pressing ahead, I tried to visualize someone walking toward me, an item of clothing or some unique ornament by which I might later recognize my spiritual teacher. The image came to mind of a large red flower.

After half an hour or so, it occurred to me that this was the first real praying I had done since my childhood, in the sense of directing a message to God while entertaining the possibility, however remote, that He might actually hear and respond. I was skeptical, but I was doing it. Not as a ritual and not for public consumption. As some Christians might have put it, I was "knocking."

But it also seemed clear that the images passing through my mind during this prayer-meditation were products of my own invention. In fact, I got up from the exercise rather disappointed that nothing whatever had been accomplished.

That evening, I stopped by a relative's house, where a distant cousin was visiting from England. I had no other information about him and no particular expectations for the encounter. But I soon learned it was no mere holiday that had brought Cousin Jeff to America. He'd come all this way to attend a "festival," at the Houston Astrodome . . . with a 14-year-old *guru* named Deva Ji!

I had seen this kid's picture on posters near the Loyola campus. In fact, he was one of the guru candidates who had come to mind during my meditation, six hours earlier. And here was my hitherto unknown cousin, commending him to me now, in terms Yogananda himself might have used: as the current *Satguru* (true teacher), whose very *job* was to open my inner eye . . . *so that I might know God for myself.* "I'm not proposing you *believe* in Gurudeva Ji," Jeff pitched me almost irresistibly. "Just give him a chance to show you what he can do. He'll either deliver or he won't."

With the benefit of a few decades' hindsight, I can picture God (or an administrative assistant) fielding my call: "What are we going to do for *this* poor guy?" They may have looked quickly around the neighborhood, spotting Gurudeva Ji in Houston and Cousin Jeff with his layover in Chicago. "This is the best we can come up with on short notice; let's just see what he'll *do* with it."

Though more than a little intrigued, I never mentioned my meditation earlier in the day nor gave Jeff any inkling what a hot prospect he had stumbled upon. As I was leaving, he handed me a magazine about the guru to take home.

I know I wasn't meditating or otherwise spiritually exerting myself as I sat there in my living room a few days later. But I felt my head begin to rotate . . . slightly, and to the left. Mechanically, in slow motion. Inexorably—of its *own accord.* Then downward just a bit, toward the coffee table . . . onto which I'd tossed that magazine from Cousin Jeff the other night.

And from its glossy cover, a portly, tuxedo-clad young man was staring up at me, mischievously. Sporting the gaudiest, most audacious *RED CARNATION* ever to have graced a guru's lapel.

Now in 20 some years of attending religious services and reciting rote prayers, I had never had such an experience. Word of other people's cosmic encounters with Gurudeva Ji added fuel to my fire, and in short order, I too was singing his praises.

But the notion of an exalted *Satguru* troubled me. This was the early '70s, and the Jesus freaks, "est"-people and followers of myriad *babas* and *anandas* (often themselves former Epsteins and Moskowitzes) all had signs and wonders of their own. It was as though there were three types of people in the world: skeptics, those who had found God and those who only *thought* that they had found Him. (And of course, the latter only made it harder for those of us in the middle category to get through to those in the first.)

Nevertheless, I continued to have extraordinary experiences that reinforced my allegiance to the guru. For example, while practicing a meditation technique called "listening to the music," strains of a Renaissance motet wafted ethereally through my right ear! The sound was so vivid, I barely made it through the first stanza before jumping up to make certain no one had a radio on in the adjacent room. (There was no radio, but after the unscheduled intermission, no more motet either.)

Another time, I became immersed in something I can only relate to the phrase "filled with the Holy Spirit." I called my wife Diane into the little, darkened hallway I used for meditation and tried to describe what I was feeling. But the sensation only quickened, outstripping any thought of running commentary. This time, it seemed right to give the experience my undivided attention, and Diane (assessing me no danger to myself or others) graciously excused me to whatever I was in the throes of.

This meditation had the feel of a tutorial—some precognitive colloquy that rose, as I tuned in, to an inspired height. I exulted there some inchoate while. And then, like the parting kiss of a spiritual lover, my reverie came into more prosaic focus.

I was working as a public defender by this time, and the upshot was a new perspective on my clients (indigent criminal defendants), on one hand, and those presiding over their due process, on the other. Years later, I tried to capture the idea part of this in a poem:

Paragons and Miscreants

Our paragons and miscreants were cut from selfsame cloth.
And equally enfranchised in the only mortal business—
that of getting (or of staying)
just as comfortable as circumstance permits.

By dint of jurisprudence drafted by my well placed peers,
our livelihood seems honest and secure.
My clients, though, must answer
for desires we can satisfy but they can ill afford.

And for us, a nonpecuniary perk:
We're seen all the more upstanding for our salutary work.
Our pride and joy; their due process . . .
All men are berated equal.

Whatever the above evokes, there was no trace of cynicism or self-reproach in the experience itself. No polemic against lawyers or some power elite, the essence of the epiphany was its very objectivity. Crowning of a bright, nonverbal piece, it was awareness, not thought—a beholding: of the ultimate innocence of every human being, however derelict his behavior.

I'm sure many people can look back on their lives and recall singular moments they felt in touch with the Divine. These may be associated with the early stage of one spiritual path or another. I once read an article by a priest, reflecting on the visitations that had called him to the priesthood. Now nearer the end of his vocation, he shared a wise hindsight that went something like this:

> Our spiritual life cannot subsist on exotic visions we may be graced to see or feel. So should you chance upon a burning bush, receive it as a sacramental boon. But then, as Moses did, get on about your Father's work. Lest *un*called for mystic pining obscure, rather than illumine your earthly path.

Lacking all such maturity, I started ranking my meditations. Then, just as fast as enlightenment had struck, I seemed to lose the meditative knack. For a while, I thought this must be some kind of test—why else would God have just stopped showing up? In my youthful ardor, it seemed only reasonable that the extraordinary, now that I'd validated its existence, should consign itself to my meditative beck and call.

Soon enough though, the press of my own worldly business had me wondering how many hours of meditation a riff of monaural music was really worth. At the risk of getting further ahead of my story, my thought today is, not very many! Perhaps the special effects are provided in the beginning as a kind of spiritual Welcome Wagon . . . after which we are called more and more (not less and less), to notice the miraculous in our everyday life and interactions.

Eventually, I made grudging peace with the inconsistency of my meditational experience, taking my spiritual pleasures where I found them. For example, I was told during my initiation ceremony that if I ever got near enough to Gurudeva Ji, I should cup my right ear and ask him for "holy breath." With that in mind, I positioned myself outside the rear entrance of a hall where the guru was speaking, hoping to catch him on his way out.

"Gurudeva Ji, could I have holy breath?" I petitioned as he came bounding toward me. With his left arm, the guru grabbed me affectionately around the shoulders. Then, curling the fingers of his right hand to form a tube, he gave a quick blow into my right ear. At that instant, I felt a corkscrew like penetration—not of air, but of some unknown medium. It was strangely nonphysical, though it did seem to enter through the ear.

Once again, the sensation was so vivid, it seems pointless to quibble over its reality (whatever I may now make of its significance). Certainly I'd been "programmed" to expect something cosmic, but what does that really explain? If a faith healer exhorts someone into a suggestible state, does that make the ensuing experience any less "real"? Looking back with this perspective, I've no good explanation for holy breath (or other phenomena we experienced as devotees of Gurudeva Ji).

Nor for a similar episode with Diane, long before I'd begun testing any spiritual waters. When she first told me she *loved* me, the very word had the same kind of penetrating effect, that time a slicing (not spiraling) into the center of my chest. As with holy breath, it was not at all uncomfortable; just vivid and completely out of the ordinary.

Our young marriage was severely tested, however, when I became a devotee of Gurudeva Ji. For though I've focused here on a few sensational experiences, it was the subtler but more consistent quality of devotion emanating from the guru's followers (but not my wife) that was winning my spiritual heart. These were people of all ages, some children and some in their eighties, who would step to the front of the room and extemporaneously express their love for God in the most personal and eloquent ways. There were no agendas, scripts or cue cards for these nightly *satsang*[3] programs. Only those who felt moved to speak came forward, and no one rushed to fill the occasional meditative hiatus.

I found the inspiration and sense of well-being at *satsang* so intoxicating, I soon was taking pains to get there for my nightly fix. Needless to say, our home life was profoundly affected by this dependency . . . and by my absence. Diane had just completed her masters in social work and taken a job as a family and child therapist. She had also started into her own psychoanalysis. Her personal and professional lives were thus orienting her 180 degrees from the direction life was taking me.

I don't recall the exchange that finally brought things to a head, but I ended up packing my bags and taking an apartment not far from my office. I shared this space with a "blissed-out" but utterly derelict devotee (whose previous address had been the woods across from Deva Ji's *ashram*). My separation from Diane didn't last more than a few weeks, however, and our reconciliation was triggered by another divine intervention I credited to the guru.

My car was in the shop, and I was sitting in the customers' lounge, reading *The Aquarian Gospel*. This book was popular among the devotees, but I couldn't seem to concentrate on it. Diane and I hadn't spoken for about a week,

---

[3] Sanskrit for "company of truth" or "holy discourse."

and my mind kept wandering to that situation. Should I call her? Should I wait for her to call me?

I paced a number of times to the pay phone on the wall. Then a rather authoritative thought occurred to me. "READ THE NEXT CHAPTER OF THE BOOK BEFORE YOU DECIDE." I sat back down, opened to exactly where I had left off and this is what I found:

Chapter 77
Jesus in Hebron. Goes to Bethany.
Advises Ruth Regarding Certain
Family Troubles.

* * *

The evening came; the multitudes were gone, and Jesus, Lazarus and his sisters, Martha, Ruth and Mary, were alone. And Ruth was sore distressed. Her home was down in Jericho; her husband was the keeper of an inn; his name was Asher-ben.

Now, Asher was a Pharisee of strictest mien and thought, and he regarded Jesus with disdain.

And when his wife confessed her faith in Christ, he drove her from his home.

But Ruth resisted not; she said, "If Jesus is the Christ, He knows the way, and I am sure he is the Christ."

"My husband may become enraged and slay my human form; he cannot kill the soul, and in the many mansions of my Fatherland, I have a dwelling-place."

*And Ruth told Jesus all; and then she said, "**What shall I do?**"*

And Jesus said: *"Your husband is not willingly at fault; he is devout. He prays to God, our Father-God.*

He feels assured that he has done the will of God in driving you away.

Intolerance is ignorance matured.

The light will come to him someday, and then he will repay for all your heartaches, griefs and tears.

And Ruth, you must not think that you are free from blame.

If you had walked in wisdom's ways and been content to hold your peace, this grief would not have come to you.

It takes a long, long time for light to break into the shell of prejudice, and patience is the lesson you have need to learn.

The constant dropping of the water wears away the hardest stone.

The sweet and holy incense of a godly life will melt intolerance much quicker than the hottest flame or hardest blow.

Just wait a little time and then go home, with sympathy and love. Talk not of Christ nor of the kingdom of the Holy One.

Just live a godly life, refrain from harshness in your speech, and you will lead your husband to the light."

And it was so.[4]

Decades later, I can hardly read this text without getting a lump in my throat. Diane was as ensconced as any Pharisee in her psychoanalytic religion. Her concern for my well-being was sincere. But like Ruth's husband, she had grown intolerant of my heresy.

However skeptical any reader may be about this incident, convinced that having subliminally glimpsed the next chapter heading, I used it as a means of resolving my ambivalence about calling Diane, I ask you to give at least my sincerity (or naivete) the benefit of the doubt. Can you imagine what it meant to me to think the guru was now interceding in my marital behalf?

I did phone Diane, and we got together about an hour later. But quite contrary to the counsel Jesus had given Ruth, I heard myself extolling Deva Ji yet again to my long suffering wife. For five seamless minutes, some trance-like *satsang* poured out of me. Only this time, Diane was taken (not turned off) by the onslaught. When I finally stopped speaking, she declared she could no longer deny her attraction to whatever was so moving me . . . or her desire to experience it herself!

I'm reminded here of the scene in *When Harry Met Sally,* where Meg Ryan fakes an orgasm in the restaurant to prove to Billy Crystal she's not sexually repressed. (A woman at the next table tells the waitress, "I'll have whatever *she's* having.")

So was this all some kind of spiritual masturbation? Was

---

[4] *Aquarian Gospel of Jesus the Christ,* by Levi (reprinted by permission of De Vorss Publications).

any part of it real? Or was it, like Meg Ryan's performance, an audacious prank? (And if so, *who* was the prankster?)

Diane did let me "lead her to the light," and she too had some memorable experiences as a devotee. But whatever spell Gurudeva Ji and I had cast on her soon began to wear off. As our relationship again deteriorated, that reversal added inexorably to my own growing doubts about the guru.

These had to do with the increasingly unrealistic burden of daily meditation (two hours for serious devotees) and nightly *satsang* of equal length; additional gatherings, wherever and whenever Deva Ji called them (like the one Cousin Jeff had come all the way from England to attend); and incessant appeals to buy the guru another car, house or helicopter!

Then at *satsang* one evening, they rolled out Deva Ji's new look. Our erstwhile *satguru* would continue to make occasional public appearances (and presumably to accept donations). But no longer was he on a mission from God. There would be no more holy breath; no more pilgrimages to his "lotus feet;" and no more nightly *satsang*. It was time for us devotees, in short, to get a life.

Overnight, Deva Ji was rebranded as a fairly ordinary young man with some meditation techniques. All the cosmic pretensions, the whole personality cult had been imposed on him (come to find out) by his now too parochial Indian flock. And apparently, his own mother . . . at whose urging back in the old country, the faithful were now flocking to the lotus feet of her more doting son, Megaditto Ji.

On hearing the above, I felt called to address my fellow devotees in a manner more lawyer-like than trance-like:

"As far as I'm concerned," I declared, "Deva Ji can carry on as *Satguru* and let the world keep right on calling him a con artist. Or he can retire comfortably and prove the world right! *Satguru* or con artist—he surely doesn't qualify for anything in between."

4

Sarah

My condition in the late '70s and early '80s was one of severe disillusionment, not knowing what to make of the above experiences and trying to limp along without a sense of spiritual direction. As alluded to above, I was now a deputy public defender, having left the large law firm that recruited me out of law school. During that first year in private practice, I had felt myself torn between my professional and devotional responsibilities and personas. But in the frenzied environment of the Public Defender's Office, I found it impossible even to feign any semblance of meditative equanimity. So after three hectic years there, I sought refuge back at Loyola Law School, teaching legal research and writing to 1st-year students.

In time I struck up a friendship with one of the faculty members I had first gotten to know as a student there. On learning of my spiritual search, he confided that he himself had been working with a psychic healer. For a while, I resisted his offer to introduce me to her, but my curiosity eventually got the better of me.

In complete contrast to the trappings (incense, pictures of the guru, etc.) that pervaded Gurudeva Ji's ashram, Sarah's home and demeanor were quite down to earth. She was a middle aged woman (like my Yoga teacher, again Jewish) who lived in a tidy Chicago suburb. Aside from a few crystals placed discreetly about her house, the scene was entirely ordinary.

But when I lay down on her couch, a strong ray of heat emanated from the hand she placed several inches above my forehead. I demanded literally to look up her sleeve, to satisfy myself she wasn't holding a small flashlight or other device.

In many sessions with Sarah over the next five years, her psychic gifts were manifest. She predicted certain events and the impact various people would be having on me. There were also phenomenological demonstrations.

For example, I once mentioned to Sarah that streetlights seemed peculiarly to be going out as I drove by. At lunch an hour later, the ceiling lamp nearest our table expired. The unruly fixture was 10 or 20 feet behind Sarah, but when I called it to her attention, she didn't turn around; she merely lowered her head and closed her eyes . . . and that light *came right back on!*

Fascinated as I was by such displays, my agenda with Sarah wasn't psychic titillation but spiritual counseling. I continued to assume there was more to life than earning a living, but whatever that might be, I certainly didn't feel connected to it. In the meantime, I could neither recreate nor explain away the intoxicating spiritual sensations I had credited to Gurudeva Ji.

Sarah served as a bridge between my inspired spiritual past and my current, workaday life. Rightly or wrongly, I didn't feel I could get what I needed from traditional psychotherapy, which seemed to lack any frame of reference for my experiences as a devotee. Neither could my family help me sort things out. (They were only glad I had stopped having whatever hallucinations had attracted me to the guru in the first place.)

But Sarah could and did reassure me that the events described above were real (if perhaps overrated). She made it clear at the outset that she herself had little use for gurus— and no interest in becoming one to me. She charged a modest hourly fee for each session. Like any good counselor, she mostly listened, giving me occasional feedback.

But where a therapist might have used my body language or choice of words to gain an understanding of my conflict, Sarah was as likely to comment on what my *aura* was doing as I recounted a particular experience. She also intuited information, sometimes with attribution to what she called "spirit guides."

Their input could be verbal, symbolic or even psychosomatic. For example, Sarah might have an acute physical reaction to something I said, the sudden cramping of a muscle, a cough, an itch or some other manifestation we would both then try to interpret. At a minimum, her physical reaction would alert us that the symptom-triggering word or phrase warranted further examination.

One such phrase, at the start of our work together, was "valuable but not gratifying." I had used it to describe some event that had benefited me professionally but that I hadn't particularly enjoyed. All my adult life, it seemed, I had felt torn between pursuits that were practical/remunerative, on one side of the ledger, and satisfying/uplifting, on the other.

This evoked for Sarah two parallel sets of railroad tracks. "It's like you're running powerful but redundant en-

gines, side by side," she commented, "an awfully ineffi-
cient way to get anywhere. Each train hauls its own cargo,
your everyday stuff here, some spiritual regalia there, as
though one were meat and the other, dairy.[5] But both are
taking you to the same place, Elliot. The tracks are *parallel*, not perpendicular."

I did feel sidetracked by those years as a devotee of Gurudeva Ji. Had I been content to remain in the ambitious
frame of mind that had served me so well as a law student,
I would have stayed at the prestigious firm that recruited
me right out of school. I'd probably be a partner there by
now, well on my way to financial security. On one hand, I
was determined not to let my penchant for soul searching
further sabotage my career. Yet I longed to re-experience
what I took to be the heightened consciousness of my early
days as a devotee.

"Show me what that *looks* like," Sarah interjected. This
took me by surprise, and in my depressed state, I doubted I
could demonstrate what it was like to be "blissed-out."
Nevertheless, I closed my eyes and began taking the slow,
deep breaths that used to catapult me into meditative oblivion. To my further surprise, I easily attained the sensation.

"You really do go way out of your body," Sarah commented. "As for the quality or 'hue' you've been pining for,
it's called 'purple.'"

"Purple?" I repeated. "What are you talking about?"

"Your aura became quite purple as you went into that
meditation. There's nothing wrong with that. Purple's a
nice, even a 'high' color. But suppose you were a painter,

---

[5] Jewish law requires a strict separation between meat and dairy
products.

standing before your easel with a palette full of beautiful colors, the entire rainbow. Yet the only one you chose to paint with was your favorite, *purple*. Don't you see how limiting this would be to you as an artist, Elliot?"

"Blue, yellow, red and green will all feel *different* than purple, but they're no less self-expressive. And they'll add immensely to your finished product if you can just incorporate them."

Sarah's words did not get me high. Nor did they resolve or even address certain psychodynamics that had caused me to play the purple/spiritual off against my other "colors." But I'll always cherish the insight she provided that day, which truly cast my conflict in a new and different light.

In subsequent sessions, we continued to work on my self-limiting notion that life and its activities were either spiritual or practical. And my all-or-nothing attitude about the validity of my experiences in either realm.

"How can it be," I persisted, "that 'God' would have taken the trouble to make contact in response to my prayer, only to lead me on such a wild-goose chase? I would never have gone down that spiritual dead-end without those extraordinary meditations, those magical coincidences . . . things that had never *happened* to me before. I don't want to talk myself out of the reality of those experiences. Yet given the frustration to which they ultimately led me, how can I *not* invalidate them?"

Sarah went silent. "I'm reluctant to repeat this," she hesitated; "you're not going to like it."

"Out with it, Sarah," I demanded.

"Well, what 'he' just said is . . . , 'Even a *flower* . . . needs *shit* to grow."

PART TWO

RELATION

5

Those "Certain Psychodynamics"

The significance of the following incident will become apparent as the story of my marriage unfolds. It occurred while I was still an undergraduate at Loyola, even before Diane and I had met. As part of my general, liberal arts requirements, I had enrolled in a beginning acting course.

At that stage of my life, I eschewed all emotional self-expression, regarding "feelings" as excuses weak people made for not having their lives together (like mine was). I conceived of actors as people who recited dialogue, throwing in a hand gesture here and a facial expression there, as necessary to make the scene convincing. Since I didn't *believe* in feelings, I certainly had no inkling what it might mean to "identify emotionally" with a particular character. I came into this class expecting simply to memorize and then "enact" (with all appropriate panache) whatever script I might be handed.

Instead, our liberal airhead of an instructor was into improvisation. He wanted us to "dig deep" and come up with "our own material." So while I waited outside the room, my classmates cooked up a scene to which my material would have to respond. All I was told by way of preparation was that I was returning home from work to my wife of several years.

I walked in on cue to discover "my wife" in bed with another man. After surveying the situation momentarily, I simply balked at playing my assigned part.

It's not that I was taken aback in any moralistic sense by the scene that confronted me. If I'd had a script, I certainly could have read the husband's lines and mustered some theatrical affect. But I lacked all capacity to identify with his predicament and *react* to it. Being so out of touch with my own feelings, I was, in the absence of canned dialogue, at a literal loss for words.

My stunted emotional condition was matched (or compensated for) by the smug assumption that my own carefully scripted life would never subject me to any such experience. No one *I* married would be capable of such a betrayal. How then could I be expected to identify with this pathetic character?

Four decades later, it's clear that my defensive armor simply didn't permit the kind of spontaneity the acting instructor was asking of me. I was one of the last to realize that my entire personality at the time was pre-scripted dialogue.

My younger brother Earl seems as cut off from his feelings today as I was at the time of my acting debut. It was in a conversation with him, not too many years ago, that the root of our emotional problem came into bold relief. Thinking myself to have matured substantially by that time, I presumed to offer my brother some feedback on *his* lagging psychological development. "I can't seem to make contact with you," I goaded. "It's like you're 'not home,' emotionally."

Earl deflected the provocation briefly before retaliating with the following jab of his own. "Don't expect me to *feel* one way or the other *about you*. I can't give you what you want. It's nothing personal; I just *do not feel.*"

I was taken aback by the incisiveness with which my brother thus cut to the chase, both of our interaction and of his psychological predicament. I asked if he had always been this way, or could he recall ever having had a "feeling"? He responded without a moment's hesitation: "I was about seven. Dad was ranting at Mother, and I was standing there, crying. 'Why is Daddy mad?' I asked. 'It's not Daddy,' Mother answered, 'it's the alcohol.'"

Earl's immediate retrieval of this incident spoke volumes to me. We'd grown up with an alcoholic father and a passive-aggressive mother. Larry would verbally abuse Ruth each night, while she made herself out to be both morally superior and impervious to the abuse. The effect of her pronouncement, "It's not Daddy, it's the alcohol," was to anesthetize my brother emotionally by *depersonalizing* the experience. In that one fell swoop, she thus severed emotional effect (and *affect*) from behavioral cause.

This may be how all psychological defenses begin. We try to protect those we love by distracting them from the source of their discomfort. But when Earl asked, "Why is Daddy mad," Daddy truly was angry. Earl found this upsetting, but he was at least in touch (*up until then*) with his own resulting turmoil.

From that day forward, however, he stopped allowing his interactions to register emotionally. Psychology calls this "denial." My father had *hurt* Earl's feelings; my mother had *relieved him of* them.

Denying or depersonalizing our pain may make sense when, as in the case of 7-year-old Earl, there's really nothing we can do about the external circumstances that are causing it. The problem is that the habit of denial robs us of the ability to enjoy improved relational conditions when they finally arrive. For subconsciously, we continue to experience life as though still confronted with whatever first put our feelings on hold.[6]

In summary, my siblings and I were taught to depersonalize the most personal of our interactions. Since it made no sense to be angry at an inanimate bottle of alcohol, Mother's implicit advice was to disregard the emotional upheaval we were experiencing on a nightly basis; to "tune out" the most dramatic events of our interpersonal lives.

Our father would then reinforce this denial by waking up stone sober each morning, as though nothing untoward had happened the night before. This was our positive male role model, strong and handsome; competent and *un*emotional. Emotion thus came to be equated in our minds with the destructive tirades "the alcohol" inflicted on us each evening. The choice seemed either to blame the alcohol (like Mother) or *become* the alcohol (like Father).

My way of dealing with my dad's verbal attacks was different from my brother's, however. I was more combative, mouthing off as much as I dared, until forced to retreat from the room or the house. I further distracted myself

---

[6] And to rationalize this muted (but now inexplicable) discomfort, we make sure to keep a supply of current-time adversity on hand. Psychology calls this "the repetition compulsion."

from this adverse home life by becoming an overachiever. As mentioned earlier, I threw myself into the B'nai B'rith Youth Organization. And between my organizational commitments, school work, choir performances and synagogue activities, I kept myself a very busy and well-adjusted looking young man.

By age 16, I was a Goldwater Republican. I went on to read Ayn Rand's *Atlas Shrugged,* with its ideologically impassioned but emotionally mute heroes. And by the time I reached that acting class at Loyola, I was acting a lot like Michael J. Fox's smug character Alex P. Keaton, in the television series *Family Ties*.

But a funny thing happened to me on my way to the Nixon White House: I met Diane. She was the antithesis of the personality I've just described: soft, warm and demonstratively affectionate. She had an innate capacity to make people feel at ease and draw them out. And it soon became her mission in life to lighten me up (which I perceived as a threat to both my Republicanism and my machismo).

I'll have more to say about Diane's dynamics later, but before continuing the story of my own emotional development, I want to fast-forward to my previously described life as a devotee. How was the carefully scripted character in the current chapter drawn, only a few years later, to the seemingly intimate and entirely extemporaneous spirituality of my cousin Jeff and his fellow devotees? How did I find the capacity, on the very heels of my acting class fiasco, to speak so movingly and *improvisationally* about Gurudeva Ji?

What I've come to understand is that these personas, the worldly/ambitious Elliot and the spiritual/introspective one, were two sides of the same coin. Like my father, I could transform myself from an extroverted but tightly controlled presentation into a state of *spiritual* intoxication. But in psychological reality, these two stances were more similar than disparate. What they had in common was their total detachment from any relational context whatsoever.

What I needed to learn was how to paint the picture of my life using more than just the purple color of passive spirituality and whatever alternative color my Michael J. Fox persona epitomized; to show my *true* colors, even as they might change from situation to situation. To correct the inconsistency between my outward appearance and what I wasn't allowing myself to *feel*. And to communicate with emotional content, not just audience pleasing theatrics.

6

Further Into the Occult

By the early 1980s, the channelers had largely supplanted the gurus at the vanguard of the New-Age. Their books were on the best seller lists, and Tanya, among others, was crisscrossing the country. When she came through Chicago, I thought about attending one of her public demonstrations. I ran the idea by Sarah, whose own channeled input was, "Elliot might find this of interest."

I should say a word about Sarah's type of channeling and how it differed from what I was about to experience. Indeed, Tanya's psychic alter ego, "Mr. Dillon," would eventually explain it this way:

> This is called "dead trance," where Tanya leaves her body and I come through. Then there's the trance where the person feels the spirit and gives the message, like a psychic reading, which can be good too.

Sarah fell into the latter category. She herself was fully present while intuiting the message. It thus remained her choice whether to pass any or all of it along. Tanya, however, claimed to be absent from her body and oblivious to what was being said by Dillon. Theirs was like a landlord-tenant relationship: The body still belonged to Tanya, but for the duration of the trance, Dillon's occupancy was exclusive.

The night I first met Tanya, she began the program by explaining the mechanics of trance as she understood them and the ground rules for how we would proceed. The lights were then dimmed and someone with a guitar began leading us in Bette Midler's "The Rose."

Tanya seated herself and closed her eyes. A moment later, her head slumped forward. We sang on, watching for the slightest telling twitch. Suddenly, the head jerked back upright and the eyes popped open. The mouth smiled, more on one side than the other. And in a strong, masculine-sounding voice, the words "FAITH AND FELICITY BE WITH YE!" rang out.

"Mr. Dillon" now spoke for several minutes on some general spiritual theme. I don't remember his specific topic that night, but we were utterly charmed by his presence. His personality, vocabulary and sense of humor were quite unlike Tanya's. (Indeed, as Dillon himself would later mention, most people found it easier to relate to *him* than to Tanya.)

We were enthralled by tales of psychic wizardry at these early trance sessions. A man who had previously asked Dillon about a problem knee now reported having awakened, later that same night, in a peculiar position—up on all fours, but with the bad leg extended behind him. And from then on, the knee had given him no further trouble.

He went on to describe a dream in which he believed Dillon had communicated with him. I was seated near the front of the room that evening, up close to Tanya/Dillon. And as the man related Dillon's dream-message, I could hear Dillon, under his breath (or Tanya's), *anticipating* it, word for word.

By the time Diane and I met Tanya/Dillon, our relationship had again deteriorated, to the point we were barely speaking. In fact, I hadn't mentioned the trance circle to her until the last moment and was surprised when she asked if she could tag along.

At first, Dillon displayed an uncanny awareness of our personalities and relational gridlock. But then he asked if we would like to be *married*. Diane politely informed him we'd been married for twelve years. "I'm talking about being married *'in the spirit,'"* Dillon replied. "Would you like to be married *by me?"*

Diane quickly took him up on the offer, her enthusiasm again catching me off guard. For all the distance between us, there had been no recent talk of separation or divorce. But neither had I contemplated re-upping, much less for multiple lifetimes. I'll digress here to explain a tenet of Dillon's teaching that was coming into play, though at the time, we were only vaguely aware of it.

He taught that each soul has an "eternal soulmate," a preordained spouse; a match literally made in heaven. Such soulmates were said to have a synergistic effect on each other's spiritual growth, such that the relational whole was greater than the sum of its parts.

Dillon thus lumped all marriages into one of two categories: *"karmic"* or "eternal." *"Karmic"* meant the pair were together to address conflicts left over from a prior lifetime. This was important work, but once the karma was resolved, the relationship had no further *raison d'etre*.

"Eternal soulmates" might well have their own conjugal karma to clean up. But in their case, the union would then blossom, not fizzle; lifting them, in the process, to their highest individual potentials.

I should mention that Tanya and Sherman always assumed until proven otherwise that any couple who came to them *were* eternal soulmates. What this meant as a practical matter was that they would be held to the high standard of marital accountability (and collective scrutiny) I'll be describing below. If this proved too difficult for either spouse, i.e., if the rigors of living life in such an intensely communicative fashion ended up driving the couple apart rather than bringing them closer together, that would show that the relationship had merely been *"karmic."*

Such couples could go on creating still more karma for each other. Or they could work diligently to resolve past and present grievances . . . and move on to find with whom they everlastingly belonged.

Diane and I were eventually converted to this vision of marriage, which became the centerpiece of our apprenticeships with Tanya/Dillon (and Tanya's own husband, Sherman). If Gurudeva Ji was supposed to have shown me how to speak to God, they would teach the two of us how to approach Him as a relationship. And how to speak to *each other*. With guest appearances by Dillon, Tanya and Sherman offered a 3-day relationship training billed as a life-changing event for the couple.

This was quite different from the spiritual counseling I had experienced with Sarah. She didn't offer conjoint sessions, nor was she focused on relational issues as such. Indeed, when I raised the eternal soulmate concept during my transition from her tutelage to Tanya and Sherman's, she took immediate exception to it. Sarah went so far as to say that from a psychospiritual point of view, Diane and I were, if anything, a *mismatch!* In all events, she rejected the idea of a preordained, "Mr. or Ms. Right" for each person and for all time.

My own experience of our 12-year marriage cast ample doubt on any thought Diane and I were meant to be together for all time. So (like any prudent lawyer attending his first trance-circle), I demanded Dillon's personal assurance that we were indeed eternal soulmates. Only then did I allow him to place his spiritual imprimatur on the relationship.

I don't remember anything out of the ordinary taking place at our nuptials the next day (except that they were being performed by a dead man, speaking through a woman's body). We repeated our vows, exchanged new rings, and I kissed the bride.

In addition to such matchmaking services, Dillon offered us individual guidance. With respect to my singing, for instance, he told me the problem was that my "throat *chakra*"[7] was closed. I asked if he could help me get it *open,* to which he replied:

> Well, one way is to tell the truth all the time and live your life in integrity. That, my son, allows for all the gifts of the spirit, which music is, to open up. But the greatest gift I can give you, Elliot, is my sense of humor! To be able to *laugh* as you sing is joyful in God, is it not? So what you have to do is come back, tomorrow, with a song to sing . . . *for me!*

Dillon then asked if we had any instruments, and someone offered up a bass fiddle they'd dubbed "Barbara." Now *Dillon* began to sing:

[7] Yogananda described the *chakras* as "occult cerebrospinal centers," the awakening of which "is the sacred goal of the yogi."

Big Brown *Babs,* she does it well!

She'll make Elliot sing, cuz he'll *go to hell*

if he *doesn't sing!* Elliot . . . El-li-*ot!*

You got a *lot,* so you better *get* it!

You think you're in *court,* when you

really need to be drinkin' *up the port!*

This cracked everyone up but me. "I really *do* want to sing," I persisted, as if the trick was just getting through to Dillon how badly I wanted it. "I've worked at this so many years, trying all the while to maintain some kind of spiritual perspective."

"Oh Gaaaaahhhddd . . . ," Dillon moaned. "*Will* Elliot be 'spiritual' *in court?* Tune in next week!" Thus did he humor us through our attachments and obsessions.

I want to turn, however, to what Tanya and Sherman, in their own flesh and blood, had to offer. They would come to town every several months to conduct what amounted to group therapy sessions, focused on our marital relationships. On the weekends in between these sessions, the Chicago group would socialize and "process"[8] together. Although we were all obviously interested in psychic phenomena and spiritual growth, we also spent time just getting to know one another.

The trance itself gradually became less the focus of our weekend soirees even when Tanya and Sherman were with us. I began to appreciate Sherman's own intuitive gift,

---

[8] "Processing" means stepping back from the task or subject at hand to deal with underlying interpersonal issues.

looking more and more to him as a kind of spiritual big brother. And there was always a sense of the psychic present to guide and inspire any of us as we processed our personal issues and relational conflicts.

During one such session, for example, I'd been unable to get in touch with anything remotely resembling a feeling (as distinguished from a thought) about what was bothering me. I had been sitting for some time against a wall, beneath a window. As my frustration mounted, Tanya's 10-year-old daughter, who was playing outside, suddenly slammed the window shut behind me. The physical jolt threw me into an immediate rage.

Tanya reined me in, stating: "My daughter is very psychic. Please do not aim your anger at her." I took this to mean the girl had somehow been guided to slam that window, thus provoking me into contact with the rage I'd been trying all morning to get in touch with. It was as if an emotional boil had just been lanced.

But within moments, the anger shifted to an overwhelming sadness. "It's my *father,*" I blurted out, not knowing why I was saying that. This led to a prolonged account of my relationship with my dad which, though not at all the focus of my earlier process, was now imbued with an emotional substance my previous sharing had entirely lacked.

It's not that I remembered any new facts about our relationship. It's just that my emotions were now reuniting with their subject matter. I was finally able to access the pain we had all known was "in there," but which I'd been unable, until that moment, to *feel*. (Such a reunion of thought and feeling, I've since come to believe, is the beginning of all emotional healing.)

For about a year, we continued our weekly get-togethers with the members of this marital support group (and with Tanya and Sherman on about a bimonthly basis). I also continued to see Sarah from time to time, and in one of those sessions, I told her Diane and I were about to spend three days alone with Tanya and Sherman, taking their "Eternal Marital Relationship Training." On hearing this, Sarah furrowed her brow and expressed some concern over what she foresaw for me at that event. "Take plenty of vitamin C," she encouraged, "and try to get a lot of rest; it's not going to be easy work."

During that same session, Sarah took me through a hypnotic, "past-life regression." I saw myself as a rabbi, married to Diane. Our relationship, as in the present, was a cold one. Diane had done something—I couldn't get the specifics, but it was in the nature of a religious or moral transgression. And I had convened a rabbinic court to address the matter, having made a firm if painful decision that my wife must be treated no differently than anyone else in the administration of religious law.

Diane never forgave what she considered my excessive show of religious principle. For the rest of that lifetime together, she was obedient but distant. Just as I had insisted on the letter of the law, so she now performed her wifely duties to the letter, but entirely without spirit.

At this point, Sarah asked me to envision our last interaction in that lifetime. I saw myself kneeling at Diane's deathbed. I was terribly repentant for the choice I had made. "If only I could go back and do it differently," I lamented, "I'd make *her* more important than any religious principle."

"Your prayer was *heard,"* Sarah interjected. "The current life is your opportunity to *make* that different choice."

My experience of this session is hard to categorize. I can't say I felt either deeply hypnotized or vividly aware of the imagery in a pictorial sense. It was more like free association than watching a movie. Yet I was having an intense emotional response as I described these scenes to Sarah. I *felt* the rabbi's profound grief at the bedside of his dying wife.

Sarah didn't alert me to any connection between all this and the "hard work" we were about to do with Tanya and Sherman. Nor did I tell them anything about the above session with her. But almost from the start of our weekend together, Sherman began prodding Diane, asking if there wasn't something she wanted to get off her chest. And she soon confirmed his intuition . . . that she had been having an affair.

I was of course devastated by this revelation. We spent the next several days filling in every bitter detail. And every other secret my wife had kept from me (or I from her). As Sarah had predicted, this was an intensely stressful emotional experience.

But through the tumultuous days and weeks that followed, I took consolation in the session with Sarah that had preceded Diane's disclosure. The Rabbi's regret—and Sarah's advice to take a different approach this time around, held out a silver lining: the possibility that real growth might result from the catastrophe, depending on how I handled it.

Diane was remorseful and begged my forgiveness. As bad as things were, there was at least a framework in place, under Tanya and Sherman's auspices, for our eventual reconciliation. Indeed, if they were right about the eternal soulmate concept, perhaps—just perhaps, the wreckage of our marriage could be hauled away and the foundation laid for a different kind of relationship. One in which I might find both the spiritual and the interpersonal substance I had long been craving.

7

Picking Up the Pieces

The total breakdown of my marriage that came to light over that weekend with Tanya and Sherman would have forced me to reassess my life and goals even if soul-searching hadn't already become for me an avocation. By now, we had been to mainstream Ph.D. and M.S.W.-type marriage counselors and Diane had been in treatment with two different psychoanalysts. Nevertheless, and despite the shambles we had made of our marriage, neither one of us seemed ready to call it a marital day.

Tanya and Sherman, meanwhile, were assuring us that the "healing" of our relationship had already begun. If we wanted to accelerate the process, they and several other couples were forming what amounted to a live-in support group for dysfunctional families. In, of all places, a town called Normal, Illinois.

They described it as a community in which, under Mr. Dillon's ultimate authority, the participants would pursue their individual spiritual development while reconstituting their marriages and family lives. It seemed a unique opportunity to turn our adversity to advantage. With one stroke, we could make a clean physical break from our sordid past and begin a new spiritual adventure.

When Sarah answered the door on my next visit, her greeting was, "Going somewhere? Come in and tell me about it." In spite of some misgivings about Tanya and Sherman, she was respectful of Tanya's psychic gift and never questioned the reality of Mr. Dillon. She also intimated that we would gain much from this experience in the wilds of Central Illinois.

For our families and friends, we tried to make the transition as respectable looking as possible. There were plenty of good reasons to be moving out of Chicago in the spring of 1983. I told my academic colleagues it was time for me to return to private practice and that I preferred to do so in a smaller-town environment. There was so much crime and traffic in the city! And with the equity we had accrued in our tiny, three-bedroom house, we would be able to afford a veritable palace in Normal. All these things of course were true, but beside the point.

Like us, the other couples moving to Tanya and Sherman's community were struggling, to one degree or another, to hold their marriages together. About half (including Sherman) were Jewish. There was another lawyer, another psychiatric social worker, a psychology professor, a medical school professor and, a bit later, a dentist. Along with our collective emotional baggage, we shared an egalitarian vision of communal living and psychological self-help.

We purchased five large homes on the same block of a nice residential neighborhood. We developed a home-schooling program for the children. The idea was to create a close-knit community in which our kids would be surrounded by a nurturing extended family. We would all feel welcome in any of the five households. And we'd be knowledgeable of and engaged in each others' personal and familial processes.

To that end, but also for economic reasons, we lived two to three families per household. For while some of us had arrived in Normal with money in the bank, the group also included waiters, delivery-people, construction workers . . . and lots of kids. As a result, our mission to save our marriages came also to entail forging community under these emotionally dire but adventuresome circumstances, across social and economic lines. Just as husbands and wives were recommitting to each other as eternal soulmates, our families were undertaking to share all aspects of the communal burden—social, psychological, spiritual and economic.

Neither Diane nor I had ever been involved in anything so radical. But we were doing this together. We were once again on the same team. And we believed that we were finally turning our dysfunctional relationship into something truly noble—not just for ourselves, but also for our 7-year-old son.

As I recall these early, halcyon days in the community, I am still struck by our bold idealism. Here we were, eventually 40 or so adults, many of us professionally if not interpersonally accomplished, committing ourselves and our resources to a common vision of marital and communal life that we were learning and inventing as we went along. We were going to help each other uproot all vestiges of selfishness, pride, deceitfulness and self-suppression. We would work diligently, within each relationship and household, to handle every interpersonal conflict and every practical challenge of daily living at the inspired level we had all experienced during our weekend sessions with Tanya and Sherman.

And for the first year or so, while we were able to live off our savings, it was truly an exhilarating experience.

8

Energy

It was a lecture by Rabbi and author Joseph Telushkin, introducing his book *Words That Hurt; Words That Heal,* that got me started writing this one. Telushkin described his subject matter as "the ethics, not the psychology" of human communication. He called for the creation of a national day on which everyone would refrain from uttering even a single harsh or hurtful word.

While my view of this has moderated in the intervening years, I still question the efficacy of a skin-deep, verbal ethic that would kosher our words without addressing our animus. For like the odorant added to natural gas, the words are but the warning smell of our more potent toxicity. And with all due respect to the Rabbi, I believe it's the toxic message (not the presentation) that should concern us.

In all events, Telushkin's focus on our verbal output (rather than the more elusive psychology and spirit of the interaction) was just the opposite of what we were shooting for in the community. For we believed the fundamental integrity of our communication, certainly in the husband and wife context, turned on the emotional authenticity with which we expressed ourselves. This made the internal conflicts and relational issues *animating* the hurtful speech more germane than the words themselves.

As though anticipating the above, the Rabbi reminded his audience that our first duty is to *behave* decently, however we may be feeling on the inside. Better to feed the hungry, even with resentment, than to hold out at their expense for some psychospiritual epiphany. The fundamental precept of *tzedaka* (righteousness) thus commands us to relieve what suffering we can and strive for a more loving spirit *(kavana)* as we go along.

Judaism thus assigns a higher value to *tikun olam* ("repair of the world") than to personal salvation. One's speech, Telushkin argues, is no less subject to this behavioral mandate. So until we can rise above our hurtful sentiments, we should find the self-control to muzzle them, at least for one day out of the year.

Of course true *tzaddikim* (righteous ones) have managed to combine the letter *with* the spirit of the law. These great souls are exalted in Jewish literature and storytelling. In *Tales of the Chasidim,* Buber recounts a student of one such *tzaddik* proclaiming, "I didn't go [to the master] in order to hear Torah from him, but to see how he unlaces his felt shoes and laces them up again." This reminds me of a statement attributed to Ralph Waldo Emerson: "I and mine do not teach by argument, but by our *presence.*"

In the psychological world, a similar debate rages between the behaviorists and the psychoanalysts. The former say, "Enough plumbing of the subconscious depths; let us clean up this patient's act!" The latter say, "Give us a few more years of treatment and we will surely get to the root of the problem. We can then effect a cure instead of just masking the symptoms."

It wasn't until I arrived at Tanya and Sherman's community that I glimpsed the possibility of integrating, in a single framework, the behavioral aspect (words and deeds) with the psychospiritual processes from which our conduct emanates. That would address a concern Diane had raised at the beginning of my spiritual search: that "spirituality" was no substitute for basic, psychological (behavioral) health. But going well beyond Telushkin's prescription, our goal was to become more fully conscious and take responsibility not just for our choice of words, but for our unspoken attitudes and agendas.

It was on this level that Tanya and Sherman perceived the real spiritual and communicative challenges to lie. They had a remarkable gift for seeing the energetic forest through the verbal/behavioral trees. To the less perceptive, this sometimes made their own behavior seem inappropriate or disproportionate.

For example, on a visit to Normal before we had decided to move there, we walked in on a heated argument between Tanya and another member of the group. Tanya became self-conscious, conflicted over whether to sweep the altercation under the rug in deference to the social expectations of the out-of-town guests. (She was well aware that to us, her remonstrations looked unseemly, if not hysterical.)

But Tanya's vehemence reflected her and the community's commitment to "call the energy," i.e., not to sit on unexpressed emotionality. They saw disrespect not in the forceful and direct exchange of angry words but in disingenuous chatter between people who were energetically pummeling one another. (That kind of socially appropriate non-communication was as offensive to them as a torrent of cuss words would have been to us.) So Tanya asked us to reserve our judgment about the intensity with which they were expressing themselves. And I professed great cool about the chaos we had intruded upon (though of course, I was politely lying through my teeth).

When things eventually calmed down, Tanya elaborated that the community's way was to respond "cleanly" but otherwise uninhibitedly to the energy of the moment. Just as soon as that energy "shifted," it would be as though the conflict had never existed. For once the energy (not just the rhetoric) had truly changed, there would literally be no grudge left to hold.

As I acclimated myself to this no-holds-barred way of interacting, I found it much more alive and honest than what passes for communication in the more polite company to which we were accustomed. I also came to agree with Tanya that the energy of conflict truly does dissipate just as soon as it's been fully and cleanly addressed—and not a moment before. The devil, of course, is in the details. But developing our attunement to energy, so as to recognize when it was "off" (in conflict) and when it had shifted (res-olution) would be a large part of our work over the next three years in Normal.

I'm sure many psychically gifted people can actually "see" this energy shift, perhaps as a change in the person's aura. Any good therapist uses his own intuitive faculties to recognize when a moment of emotional reality breaks through the chatter of ordinary defensive banter; when the defenses have been sufficiently penetrated to allow both the consciousness and the behavior to truly change. Whether we speak in psychological or psychic terms, the process is the same. The person finally "gets" (realizes) that small piece of his life's puzzle, and the air is somehow, almost miraculously, cleared.

This differentiation between words and their underlying

energy did not come easy to me, however. Indeed, I dismissed it at first as so much New-Age psychobabble. Not surprisingly, this soon created tension between me and the group. They accused me of concealing my own hostility behind lawyer-like words and convincing arguments. And for an excruciating time, I really had no clue what these people were talking about.

An early incident will illustrate just how out of touch I was. Just a few days after moving to Normal, I found myself in a room with Sherman and two of the men, engaged in some rather lively if egotistical banter about the great spiritual things we were going to do together. I made some comment I no longer recall that evoked from Sherman an affectionate if slightly teasing response: "Oh, am I such a heavy *burden* to you?" And without the slightest conscious awareness of any hostility toward Sherman, I retorted, "Not a heavy burden . . . just *FAT.*"

Seeming stunned, Sherman stood up and walked slowly out of the room. A hush fell over the three of us who remained, but was quickly broken when Tanya came flying in . . . and ordered me to *leave the house!*

I left, shaken, apologetic and profoundly confused. An emissary soon came to inform me that I would be unwelcome in Sherman's household until my energy had "shifted." In the meantime, I was to communicate with him and Tanya only through third parties!

I'll not address here the disproportionality of this response to my teasing quip (or the kind of communal power structure it revealed). What I want to focus on for the present is the reality of the energetic body blow I had in fact delivered to Sherman; and what he and Tanya had to teach me about energy.

I was told the offense was particularly heinous because it came as such a sneak attack, at a time we appeared to be just relaxing and enjoying each other's company. For days I protested my motivational innocence. Unfortunately, these people only viewed "I'm sorry *if* what I said hurt you" as rubbing salt in Sherman's wound. The energy remained to be dealt with until I not only admitted but "got" the intentionality (even if unconscious) of my snide remark.[9]

How often do we experience well-meaning apologies that fail to inspire any confidence the offending behavior won't soon be repeated? This isn't necessarily because the apology is insincere. It's because the energy, as distinguished from the behavior, hasn't been identified much less corrected. Thus, until I could get in touch with (actually *feel*) my hostility toward Sherman, any regret I might express could only be for the adverse consequence *I* was now suffering as a result. (Meanwhile, the energy would lie in wait for another opportunity to ambush him . . . or someone else.)

Now even as thick as I was in the spring of 1983, I could not long deny that my sarcastic remark about Sherman's weight was tactless. After some soul searching, I "got" that it was a tad provocative. But the entire fabric of my self-image balked at any notion of actual malice. (Had my mother been there, *she'd* have spoken up for me: "Oh, Sherman, you're making a mountain out of a molehill. You're too sensitive!")

But something Sherman had said, just before walking

---

[9] However paradoxical, my eventual realization that our behavior is no less intentional when it *is* unconscious was a personal breakthrough for which I will always be indebted to Tanya and Sherman.

out of the room, stayed with me. Giving no hint of the ax that was about to fall, he had muttered something about a "feminine energy." Then standing, and with more conviction, he declared: *"That* was a woman!" Which utterance somehow evoked for me not my mother's, but my *sister's* inflection, each time I replayed the tape of what had just slipped out of me.

Now a therapist, looking back with me on this incident, might have probed his way to the association between my behavior on this occasion and my sister. The sudden verbal jab was her trademark in our nightly skirmishes with "the alcohol." But Sherman's insight was spontaneous, not reflective. He didn't deduce my sister's influence; he *felt* (intuited) it.

Of course it was my energy (not my sister's) that had taken this potshot at him. But this unexpected linkage to her (and to the cutting sarcasm with which she fended off our father) eventually brought me around to the more pertinent question: What was *I* now lashing out against (*or fending off*)?

If all this seems too complicated, paranormal or far-fetched, we could just say that I had learned from my sister a style of fighting that I had just unleashed on Sherman— for reasons that were yet to be identified. We all borrow in this way from our siblings and parents to perpetuate our distinctive family brands of what Rabbi Telushkin calls "hurtful speech." But to the extent I might have attempted to pass the responsibility off to my sister (or my mother), they (or their therapists) could just as easily have referred me farther up the ancestral chain. For every such familial legacy awaits a generation with the fortitude to say, "Enough is enough. The neurotic buck stops here. I (and my *children*) shall be free of this."[10]

I do believe my personal growth, and my children's, was thus accelerated because Tanya and Sherman did for us what no proper therapist would or could have done. Through the interactive rough and tumble of this "spiritual community," they subjected themselves (and *their* children) to the unfiltered onslaught of my displacement, along with everyone else's.

Experienced therapists know that their patients' transference[11] can and will exploit any weakness in their professional armor. That's another reason they don't invite the patient home for tea (much less move him into the spare bedroom, as Tanya and Sherman were doing). They don't share their own hopes, fears and frustrations, lest the patient find a way to use that information against them (or to sabotage the treatment).

Tanya eventually explained that only moments before my quip about Sherman's weight, he had confided to her his increasing self-consciousness *on that very score*. Now Sherman wasn't obese, and it had not entered my *conscious* mind that he might be sensitive about his weight. But that doesn't mean I didn't *intuit* the sensitivity. Sherman and I, in short, were equally psychic: I, by knowing where he was vulnerable; he, by sensing my cheap shot had something to

---

[10] This should not be confused with the defiant energy psychology calls a "reaction formation" (where we make a point of doing just the opposite of what our parent(s) would have done or wanted). That knee-jerk and entirely behavioral strategy only reinforces the emotional legacy we think we are rejecting.

[11] The patient/client's tendency to transfer or displace his unresolved parental conflicts onto the therapist.

do with how the women in my life had influenced me. I doubt any therapist could have gotten the ball rolling more quickly.

In a nutshell, the concept of energy, as taught by Tanya and Sherman, meant we owed a duty—at least to those we claimed to *love*—to *become* more fully conscious. To take responsibility not just for our words and behavior, but for the effect our very *presence* is having on those around us.

Based on this high standard, the community served as an extension of the eternal soulmate relationship. Indeed, we began to speak less of "community" and more of "spiritual family." The idea, or ideal, was to extend the same high level of responsibility for our spoken and *unspoken* communication outward, from the nuclear family to the larger spiritual one; and eventually, even to the stranger on the street.

For that, we felt, would be the beginning of real *tikun olam*.

9

Spiritual Community

What roles, then, were we playing for each other in this unusual psychospiritual enclave? We weren't "friends" in the normal sense of that word. There was a definite hierarchy, with Mr. Dillon presumably at the top and Tanya and Sherman taking care of the day-to-day administration of the collective energy. There were also designated "heads of household," who were the initial arbiters of what was going on among the residents of each house.

The organizational structure and spiritual aliveness somehow reminded me of the Children of Israel on their departure from Egypt. We believed we had left the bondage of our moribund relationships and psychic ignorance in Chicago, Denver, Philadelphia or wherever we had come from. We looked to Tanya and Sherman to guide us through the uncharted relational wilderness. And we counted on an unseen higher authority to intervene, whenever we might lose our collective-intuitive way.

As suggested above, the commitment to the eternal soulmate was the covenant upon which the social and philosophical structure of the community rested. The marital relationship was seen as both the context and the catalyst for the psychospiritual growth of the individual (and of the group as a whole). We continued to draw inspiration from

Tanya's weekly trance, but it was in the small and large conflicts and energy shifts to which the grist of daily living subjected us that we waited on the Lord.

Our lives were thus filled with myriad small moments of interpersonal truth. Our psychospiritual classroom was the kitchen, the work place, the bedroom—wherever we found ourselves. We made no distinction between neurotic, relational and spiritual issues, believing that any of these, if examined with courage and determination, would lead us to the Truth. We likewise assumed that our familial and communal conflicts, if handled with integrity, would bring to light and help resolve our most deep-seated individual pathologies.

The Eternal Soulmate Relationship:
"It Guards Your Breath As It Cleans Your Teeth"

Early in our marriage, we knew a couple who could have been Mr. and Mrs. Jack Sprat. He was thin as a rail, and she was morbidly obese. She then underwent a gastric bypass procedure (at that time, still largely experimental). The operation was a success but the relationship died. She dropped over 100 pounds; then he dropped her!

It seems self-evident that any significant change in the individual is going to impact the relationship. Is it not incongruous, therefore, for marriage counseling and individual treatment to be administered as separate disciplines? The therapist treats the individual without input from the absent but no less impacted spouse; while the marriage counselor addresses the couple's communication, but with scant attention to root psychological issues.

We were thus enthused about combining the work of the therapist and the marriage counselor in a single venue. We believed if we were to make real and lasting progress as a couple, it would be necessary to identify and address the individual neuroses that were driving the relationship. At the same time, we felt that our individual issues were best accessed through the relationship, since that's where they most pervasively presented. Finally, we had accepted the theory that the marital relationship (with the eternal soul-mate gloss added) provided not only the arena but the spiritual catalyst through which the individuals would achieve their emotional healing.

Healing the Relationship: The Medium Is the Message

What is the goal of psychotherapy? Unlike other forms of education, its highly personal curriculum aims specifically at self-knowledge. Nor is it merely an intellectual study. Our increasing self-awareness marks our progress toward emotional and spiritual maturity.

But just as our psychospiritual deficiencies reveal themselves in our behavior, shouldn't individual growth likewise manifest functionally, in *improved* behavior and relationships? For what good is self-awareness if it doesn't help our relationships work better?

I'm reminded here of a conversation many years ago with a med-student friend who was planning to become a psychiatrist. He had a surprisingly cynical attitude about his future career, shaped apparently by his own experience as a patient. "My therapy didn't work," he bluntly told me.

"What it achieved," he continued, "was the identification of my emotional issues, but without any real impact on them or their relational consequences." His devastatingly negative conclusion was that we neither feel nor behave better after therapy; we simply earn the dubious privilege of knowing just what we're *doing* to our loved ones and ourselves!

Under the eternal soulmate rubric, by contrast, our vision of emotional health was entirely functional. The relationship served as our psychological proving ground.

But what does "work better" *mean* in the marital context? Many couples are content not to rock the boat—to maintain the emotional complementariness that attracted them to each other in the first place. Whereas homing in on the individual energies fueling the couple's conflict tends to *de*stabilize the relationship, at least as presently constituted.

Nevertheless, our idea of improved communication was not the avoidance of overt conflict at the cost of keeping it covert. In that sense, we saw marital friction as the coin of the therapeutic realm—not to be shortchanged into tidy but less evocative "I-statements."

We also knew that regardless of whose behavior appeared to have "started" the particular conflict, there had to be some concomitant individual issue at play within the spouse, inciting him or her to engage in the drama, i.e., to take the proffered neurotic bait in the first place. This fight wouldn't be happening—this couple *would not be together,* were they not in some symbiotic emotional cahoots.

We realized, in short, that what defense mechanisms are to the individual, the relational status quo is to the couple. Just as we deny our internal conflicts in a vain attempt to preserve our personal comfort, so the relationship constructs an interlocking network of defenses, looking thereto for some modicum of stability. But as the effect of denial is to cut the individual off from his feelings, so the neurotic symbiosis erodes the couple's capacity . . . for *intimacy*.

We recognized, finally, that all marital conflict is at once a symptom of and a railing against this very symbiosis. When an argument erupted, we saw it as one or the other spouse's thrust (however unconscious) for *greater* intimacy—a conjoint version of the repetition compulsion. The first step was to identify which partner was thus stirring the neurotic pot on this conflictual occasion.

Our purpose wasn't to referee the conflict or to declare one side "right" and the other "wrong." The object was to identify the person who was, in reality, calling attention to his own (individual) issue; so that it could be addressed. As we would put it, that person's energy "was up."

The Eternal Soulmate's Carrot

We believed, with all the fervor of religious acolytes, that each partner had both the capacity and the spiritual duty to help heal the other. For the spouse could do two things the therapist could not: He could *love* the "patient"; and be there for the long haul.

I'm a big fan of Carl Rogers, but his famous claim of "unconditional positive regard" for his clients has always baffled me. Is the "regard" not metered out in 45-minute increments, and at $150 per dose? I don't begrudge any therapist his livelihood, but "unconditional" such regard is not.

We, on the other hand, had vowed to love each other for richer or for poorer, in sickness and in health. And as eternal soulmates, we now sweetened the package with a lifetime emotional benefit: By communicating ever more cleanly, ever less defensively, we would *love* our way to the bottom of every conflict, unraveling and dissipating, in the process, wounds and grievances from our distant individual pasts.

The Eternal Soulmate's Stick

But we also saw the marriage contract as a license to call (confront) the energy whenever we sensed something, behavioral or *pre*-behavioral, disturbing our own equilibrium. As the one who bore the brunt of our partner's neurotic habit, we considered it both our right and our duty to initiate process. In sharp contrast to the therapist's more passive objectivity, our job was precisely to *personalize* every marital interaction, to insist our spouse take notice of her energy's impact *on us;* to thereby make our presence—and through it, every latent (individual) conflict—truly felt.

That meant never hesitating to probe our partner's defenses in order to give our love the chance to do its healing work. As suggested above, we saw this as the growth-demanding ingredient that was missing from the professional therapeutic relationship.

Of course, doing this cleanly, i.e., knowing *whose* defenses were actually asserting themselves on any given occasion, was much easier said than done. For in establishing the relational homeostasis, we had learned precisely how to push each other's neurotic hot-buttons. Our psychospiritual mission, to express more love and less pathology, thus became, by definition, an ongoing exercise in self-examination. It was in this way that our individual and relational processes truly catalyzed one another.

For we were determined to do more than just identify our neuroses. We were going to *grow* ourselves *and* the relationship. Or move on to find the one with whom we might realize such individual and relational synergy.

10

Sexual Energy

A passage in the Talmud reads, *"Da lifney mi ata omeyd* -- Know (be aware) before Whom you are standing." This text often appears in the synagogue, on or near the Ark that houses the sacred Torah scrolls. It teaches that we should live our lives as though *always* standing before the Holy Ark, i.e., knowing that our every act and thought are fully open to God's view.

It was on our initial visit to the community, before we had decided to move to Normal, that I was confronted with the practical implications of standing not before God, but before someone with a paranormally intimate view of me. "Take your filthy hands off my daughter and *keep* them off!" Tanya upbraided me.

Now I hadn't physically touched Tanya's attractive teenage daughter but was as guilty as Jimmy Carter of the lustful thought. This rebuke was my notice Tanya ran a tight ship when it came to sexual energy in particular. Since most of us were used to giving our fantasies free rein, her psychic sensitivity on this score made us nervous and kept us vigilant.

The realization that our sexuality could be observed, even in the absence of the slightest verbal or behavioral "come on" cast a whole new light on our social mores. We began to notice how much sexual communication takes place long before rising to the level of suggestive speech or body language. Our liberated culture has gone almost completely unconscious in this regard. As Dillon used to put it, the same man who might shoot you for touching his car thinks nothing of it when you dance cheek to cheek with his wife!

But Tanya's zero tolerance for energetic smut was practical, not prudish. Considering the level to which we were holding each other accountable, we could hardly have overlooked foreign sexual incursions into the eternal soulmate relationship. And it would have been the height of duplicity to ask another member of the group to lower his emotional guard enough to process with me . . . while I was entertaining sexual fantasies about his wife!

Or to be having sex with my own wife while thinking about someone else's. Indeed, we considered it the spouse's job to ferret out any such energetic philandering. If my partner didn't know (or care) where my consciousness was, so long as my sex organ was present and accounted for, *both* of us were being energetically unfaithful. For our goal was to stop using anyone as a sex object, from the total stranger to our own spouse.

In the case of the spouse, that might mean initiating process even at the cost of *coitus interruptus*. In the case of an attractive young stranger, it meant envisioning her mother and father standing right there beside her; loving her in a more personal way than I might, in their absence, have been inclined to.

"Da," they'd be saying if I would only hear them. "Know before *Whom* you are standing."

11

Group Psychoanalysis

Diane's experience in psychoanalysis made this consolidation of individual, conjoint and group modalities all the more attractive to us. I'll digress here to describe the psychoanalytic model of emotional healing, as I've come to understand it.

The analyst (usually an M.D. psychiatrist) "treats" the patient in an interpersonally sanitized, clinical environment. Lying on a couch, the patient free-associates (says whatever comes to mind) with a minimum of direction from the analyst. The idea is for the patient, over time, to get in touch with his innermost fantasies and preoccupations.

The analyst, by contrast, remains scrupulously *im*personal in these sessions. Seated behind the patient like an invisible alter ego, he offers sporadic interpretive comments the substance and timing of which are what make the process a therapeutic one. But like any good clinician, the analyst must monitor the patient's process from a personal/relational remove.

There's good reason for this professional detachment. The symptomatology of the patient's "illness" is his history of unsatisfactory interactions with family, friends, employers, etc. However well handled the analyst's own issues and relationships might be, were he to allow his emotional field to intersect the patient's, he would become part of the very subject matter he was trying to help sort out. To prevent this, the analyst takes pains to avoid contact with the patient outside their formal sessions. He likewise cordons himself off from the patient's family and friends, in order to maintain both complete confidentiality and undivided loyalty to the patient.

The analytic hour thus amounts to an interactive time-out, a freeze-framing of emotionally charged events for review and interpretation with the analyst before pushing the relational resume-play button. To that end, *both* participants are sequestered from their respective personal contexts for a most private, but relationally sterile *tete a tetè*.

Now I didn't know any of the above in the days of Diane's first psychoanalytic experience. However, all the signals my wife was sending suggested that her treatment was not going well. Over a period of months, she had become increasingly depressed, to the point that she was now talking, albeit abstractly, about *suicide*. When this got me concerned enough to begin hiding away my razor blades, I took it upon myself to phone her analyst.

Dr. Heinrich spoke to me in terms even a psychologically illiterate young lawyer like me would comprehend. "Sir, you and I do not have a contract. My contract is with your wife. I cannot discuss this matter with you. So please do not interfere any further in my work with Diane."

Even with my current understanding of the importance of confidentiality in the psychotherapeutic relationship, this response to my legitimate if unsolicited concern still strikes me as doctrinaire and overzealous. In all events, my reaction at the time was to give Diane an ultimatum: "You can have your 'work' with that man or your marriage with me. If the good doctor interprets my call under these circumstances as an interference with *his* contractual expectations, one of us has got to go."

Thus forced to choose one authority figure over the other, Diane chose me. The implications of this will be addressed in a later chapter, but the above may shed further light on the appeal that Tanya and Sherman's approach had for both of us. For in their community, there was no turf war between the individual and relational processes. The relationship was seen as the very portal to the psychodynamics of the individual. Whatever issues needed to be addressed, it was within the relationship that they would inevitably present. We could then work backwards, from the patent marital conflicts to the more latent individual ones.

Tanya and Sherman were thus taking a systems approach, examining the individual issues in their larger, relational context. But unlike even a systems-oriented therapist or marriage counselor, they had on-the-spot access to the relationship and its constituents. If a conflict erupted at midnight, we would all roll out of bed and lend our collective insight to its resolution. And *stay* with the process, not for 45 minutes, but until the energy at play had been identified and, hopefully, had shifted.

Needless to say, this created quite a different culture than the one we had all grown up with. In normal married life, husbands and wives attempt to address their conflicts, if at all, in private. So long as the marital *behavior* remains within bounds, the relationship muddles through its ups and downs, maintaining discretion while on public display. An unfinished argument on Saturday afternoon may thus give way to convivial chitchat as the dinner guests arrive. Unless and until the pair can no longer keep the lid on, they will endure this marital Jekyll and Hyde routine, relating to each other one way when they're alone and quite another (like a set of dress clothes) for public consumption.

In the community, we came to disparage the latter as "performance behavior." Our goal was to walk our domestic talk, to live up to the authenticity we espoused, not just at home but in our social and even economic contexts.

But we didn't *do* much socializing outside our immediate circle. And economically, we were largely resting on our collective, if fast-dwindling laurels. In short, we had retreated from the very settings that tend to call for performance behavior in the first place.

In the vernacular of personal boundaries, we had all but erased them among ourselves but erected a firm, parochial one between us and the world at large. Like provoked bees, we would swarm in at the first sign of non-communicative backsliding within our ranks. (We considered this a form of communal "tough love.") But in the larger scheme of things, we had severed the umbilical cord of socioeconomic accountability that makes life on earth what it is.

I recall one time we did venture out into the real world. Through an acquaintance on the faculty at Purdue, Diane and I were invited to lead a 10-week pilot program of group therapy for couples. This was under the auspices of the University's Center for Family Studies. The project went so well, several of the couples wanted to keep working with us after the formal program had ended. So we began seeing them at our home, on a weekly basis.

Unfortunately, one of the true zealots of the community

took a reading of our energy and concluded we were becoming uppity in our new roles. Our home office was a room that served, when we weren't meeting with the outsiders, as passageway to the laundry room. Unwilling to be inconvenienced by the airs she perceived us to be putting on, this woman came barging through one of our sessions with her basket of dirty underwear (giving a whole new meaning to "airing our dirty linens").

We should have realized then that the gap between the community's uncompromising agenda and the demands of life in the real world was too great to bridge; that authenticity and discretion weren't mutually exclusive, personal boundaries not an all-or-nothing proposition; and that communication could be both honest and sincere without being unremittingly self-revealing or conflictual.

12

Here a Psychic, There a Psychic

At one introductory trance circle, a young woman asked Dillon if he could help her become a famous photographer. "You're already famous *with me*," Dillon quipped; "I don't know what more I could possibly do for you in the fame department."

Dillon never encouraged our thrust for personal status, much less fame. He posited "ego" as our spiritual nemesis and exhorted us to "overcome" it. [12]

I was thinking about this one day as I waited at the Department of Motor Vehicles to renew my license. After 20 minutes in line, I got close enough to the counter to read that the renewal fee had gone up, from $4 to $7. I had $6 in my pocket . . . and my checkbook. But the sign also announced that they had stopped accepting checks.

It was a hot summer day and I was tired and fed up. The last thing I wanted to do was drive all the way home and back, just to wait another 20 minutes in line. In my prior, more dignified life, there would have been no alternative.

But my ruminations about ego suddenly ripened into a

[12] I use "ego" (as did Dillon) in the colloquial, not the Freudian sense.

bold if unconventional action plan: Why not ask one of the 50 other patrons in line to save me an hour's time by lending me the dollar I was short? I could then write *them* a personal check (or take their address and mail the dollar right back to them).

The thought of doing this threw me into immediate agitation and embarrassment. Was my resistance to so practical a solution something I should endeavor to "overcome"? I took a deep breath, turned to the person behind me in line and began describing my predicament.

A woman standing distinctly off to the side quickly pulled a dollar from her purse and rushed over with it. When I began to write her a check, she emphatically put up her hand, stating: *"I have been told* that I should give you this money, that it's important. Under the circumstances, it wouldn't be right for me to accept your check."

Now it could just be that a disproportionate percentage of Normal's population *isn't*. But I preferred to take meaning from what had just transpired: that Dillon (or some other privy to my internal process) had gotten the attention of my flesh and blood benefactor. Who in turn was willing to underwrite a buck's worth of my spiritual education.

More was accomplished here, in my estimation, than the avoidance of a drive home to get the extra dollar.

13

"The Universe Will Provide"
(and Other Euphemisms of Denial)

Experiences such as the above convinced me that virtually any interaction could serve either to dilute or to reinforce my identification with ego. When I hid my distress from those who hurt me, I chose defensiveness over honest communication. When I allowed the fear of rejection to deter me from asking for help, I fostered ego at the expense of relationship and faith in God.

But this seemed a slippery slope. Was there not a line to be drawn between faith and humility, on one hand, and slothful dependency on the other? Otherwise, what kept us all from just plunking ourselves down in some comfortable spot, with a sign reading, "Vulnerable. Need Cash. God Bless"?

We did that for a while in a manner of speaking. It wasn't as if we hadn't put our own hard earned money where our spiritual mouths were. But somewhere along the way, we lost sight of the fact that neither our marriages nor our spirituality existed in a physical (or fiscal) vacuum. Compounding the error, as our cash and credit resources dwindled over months of non-remunerative interpersonal process, we became self-righteous about our very willingness to turn to others for help.

I remember, for instance, a conversation with a fellow who had attended a number of the early Chicago trance circles. Brian had stopped short of moving with us to Normal but had generously lent $5,000 to Ed and Jessica to help them make the move. Now, reasonably enough, he wanted to be paid back. And since the debtors were living in my house, it fell to me, as head of household, to monitor the financial and interpersonal heat we were starting to get.

So on Brian's next visit to Normal, I arranged a sit-down for the four of us. He opened the discussion with a rendition of his new mantra, "a contract is a contract." We of course weren't interested in the law of contracts but in the deeper energies at play.

I told Brian there were two ways we could approach this conversation. "Contractually speaking," the debtors had a duty to repay the money, and he had every right to collect it (rights and duties being the correlatives of such obligation-driven, i.e., legal relations). But Ed, Jessica, Diane and I had moved beyond such bourgeois concerns to a more personal (if all but unenforceable) "commitment"-driven relationship. This meant we had stopped focusing on the petty details of who owed what to whom in favor of a richer interactive process.

Into which I was now inviting Brian, also, to step. The closing pitch went something like this:

> We can sign a formal agreement, by which we'll undertake to pay you so much per month, for so many months. If we then don't live up to those terms, you can get right back in line with our other creditors . . . or file your lawsuit.

Or we can give you the kind of commitment we've made to each other. The essence of which is, we're accountable [another spiritual term of art] for what we do each day and how we disburse the financial fruits thereof. Were you to become part of that ongoing discussion, we would owe you a real voice in our deliberations, financial and otherwise.

We would then welcome you into our soul-searching as to which financial need is most compelling at any given moment (not just on the monthly basis we deal with our creditors). But I have to warn you that engaging with us in that ongoing process could get you paid back sooner or it could get you paid back even later than if we go the route of contractual obligation. The difference is that accountability addresses *all* our needs and resources—*yours included*. But under the obligation scenario, the $5,000 Ed and Jessica owe you will delimit your relationship—with them and with the *rest* of us.

The upshot was, Brian gave up on being our creditor to become our spiritual relative.

Yet I was also willing to play the patsy of my own spiritual fast-talk. There was the time Tony and Lisa were living in our house, with their 3-year-old daughter and another child on the way. Tony had just gotten a job at the post office, sorting mail on the graveyard shift. I had encouraged him to apply for that job. In fact, I had put up the money for the course that got him through the qualifying exam; and for the new tricycle his little girl had her heart set on for Christmas.

But at dinner one cold January evening, Tony shared with us how much he was already hating the new job. He threw in that his coworkers had begun plying him with amphetamines, just to get him through the nightly shift.

Now I had known this young man since moving to the community and did feel a sense of commitment to him and his family. But it was our mortgage, not theirs, inching closer to foreclosure. So what I felt like saying was:

YOUR JOB SATISFACTION IS NOT MY PROBLEM. *LIFE'S A BITCH!* SO **STRAIGHTEN UP AND FLY RIGHT**. And I had better see your family's share of our expenses, without fail, on the 15th!

But before I could get that out, I happened to glance at his little girl, playing serenely on the floor with our own toddler-son. Those two were inseparable. I couldn't help but imagine the turn her life might take were her daddy to get hooked on speed.

"To hell with that job," I heard myself saying. "We'll figure out another way for you to bring in some money."

During this confusing time, I learned what it was like to walk into a supermarket and see items I wanted to buy but couldn't afford. One day, I was in Chicago filing a brief when I realized I might not have enough *gasoline* money to make it back to Normal. "I can't live this way," I whined that evening. "I'm a *lawyer*, for Christ's sake. I shouldn't have to hassle over whether it takes $2 or $3 worth of gas to get me home from court!"

Tanya glared at me. *"All my life,"* she seethed, "I've been 'hassling' over things like that. What's it *like, Mr. lawyer,* driving into a gas station and just saying, *'fill 'er up'?"*

Heading back to Chicago a week later, I was pleased to discover that I had money for gas and for lunch in the bargain. "Where shall I eat?" I asked myself. "Chinese sounds good," came the answer. "If you pass a Chinese restaurant, PULL IN."

Seconds later, I spotted the New Hong Kong Buffet, a place I had never tried. As I entered, there seated at the table just in front of me was my erstwhile boss and current part-time employer, Jack Murphy.

Now I had known and worked for Jack for several years, but never shared a meal alone with him. He seemed preoccupied and rather somber. Taking some liberty, I asked him what was up. "It's a money thing," he cryptically replied.

Flashing back to my recent experiences with creditors and at the Department of Motor Vehicles, I matter-of-factly suggested Jack just come right out with his predicament to whatever employees or business associates stood to be affected. Making a great leap which, in my spiritual oblivion, seemed like no leap at all, I said, "If the firm was a *family,* you'd just round us all up and say, 'Uncle Jack's got a problem.'"

Jack seemed to shrug off the suggestion. But I left that restaurant no less puffed up, convinced that *God* had sent me there to deliver a spiritual message; that I had just done, for Jack Murphy, what the woman at the DMV had done for me.

14

Whom Do You Love?

At one trance circle, I told Mr. Dillon I was feeling confused about life's purpose . . . and more particularly, my own. I wondered what I was missing, or if I was even asking the right questions.

"Do you love your wife?" Dillon responded, seeming to change the subject. "Yes," I answered after a brief pause. "Then what else is there to ask . . . or to know?"

The ultimate purpose of life, Dillon seemed to be saying, was to love, not in some abstract, agape sense but in relation to another specific human being. His spiritual teaching thus differed from the Eastern philosophies I had encountered. The latter discouraged relational entanglements, viewing them as distractions from what should be the aspirant's single-minded yearning *for God.*

But Dillon posited relationship as an ideal venue within which to develop our spirituality. He saw the householder's worldly responsibilities as a natural hedge against selfishness. Our very entanglements should help inoculate us against hedonism, preventing sensation from drowning out all receptivity to the needs of our significant others.

My own father sired four children and was married to the same woman for 51 years. But he never repented of his hedonism. When the issue of his drinking occasionally came up, his defense was that he didn't "have" to drink, but rather *"chose"* to.

Now did the fact that he could even say such a thing to us mean he didn't *"love"* us? Or was he "doing the best he could"? And did our willingness to continue interacting with him, long after we had reached ages at which we had a say in the matter, mean we loved him more than he loved us? Or were we codependent gluttons for punishment, no less *choosing* to remain in relationship with him than he was still choosing his alcohol over us?

We all put up with more mistreatment from family members than from a stranger on the bus; more from our boss than our neighbor. The question always reduces to, "What have we to gain and what to lose by the continuation or termination of this relationship?"

Most of these deliberations are subconscious. But one interaction with my father, shortly before we left the community, taught me to deal more forthrightly with the perennial question, "Is this relationship redeemable? Should I risk further pain for the *possibility* of experiencing love with this person?"

My 1983 taxes were in arrears, and the IRS had now placed a $7200 lien on our house. I knew my dad had some money saved up; what about asking *him* for some help?

The likelihood of a positive response seemed remote, that of a contemptuous rebuke all but certain. But it had been a long time since I had asked Dad for anything (other than to sober up). Suppose I were to approach him, this time, about *my* predicament instead of his own; with the same kind of straightforwardness I had mustered for the patrons at the department of Motor Vehicles.

There was a big difference, of course, between that inter-action and the one now under consideration. My father and I had a history. It's probably easier to stand on the corner and beg from strangers than to confront our more personal demons by approaching "our own" for help.

But the good fairy was nudging me to take this risk—to give my dad and myself one more opportunity to grow, both individually and relationally. Her challenge went something like this:

What if God is standing by, ready to support (but not initiate) a miracle. Waiting to give your father the gentle boost he needs if you can just approach him nonjudgmentally. With the common respect he's not been shown in years, especially by a member of his own family.

Imagine the potential healing if he could then find the wherewithal to part with some of his false secu-rity. Not because he "had" to; not because you de-manded it. Because he *chose* to. Because in the light of your vulnerability, his love surged ahead of his fear.

And think what such an outcome would mean to you, Elliot. Getting the IRS off your back would be the least of it. This *isn't* some stranger at the DMV, this one is *your* daddy (who already *is* addicted). But that sober reality need not deny you or him the oppor-tunity to rise to this occasion.

"Don't be a shmuck," the bad fairy cut in. "Beggars stand on street corners because 'phoning home' would be like banging their heads against a stone wall. You'd be smarter to go out and get your own tin cup than to call your dad; you might actually raise some cash! In all events, the rejection of a passing stranger would be a lot less painful than one more kick in the teeth from *that* asshole."

The good fairy won. I made the call. My dad was sober; so far, so good. I spoke with more emotional authenticity than I had shown him since my early childhood. And he listened with uncharacteristic patience.

After a few moments, Dad said, "Here's what I want you to do. You call the IRS and arrange to pay them $300 a month for the next two years. I can't give you any of my saved-up money, but I'll send you half my Social Security check, and you can use that to pay off the IRS."

That conversation was a miracle I will always cherish. But in the mail a few days later came the following, on a *postcard:*

> I can't do it. It's not that I don't *love* you.
> Please understand.

I burst into tears when that postcard arrived. But I also realized the above communication was a second miracle, equal to the first. It had been a long time since my dad and I had offered our best to each other; since we had both found the wherewithal to acknowledge our love . . . in the very *face* of our limitations.

15

Our Most Reckless Leap of Faith

Diane and I lived through three pregnancies together. Our first son was born by cesarean section, after three intense days and nights of labor. There was no obstetric reason for the difficulty. She had sailed through the pregnancy, the picture of radiant expectancy. Neither her pelvis nor the size or position of the baby posed any impediment. She just would not dilate.

It seemed not to have affected son #1, but Mom was certainly traumatized by the experience. Within a few months, she had slipped into a post-partum depression so severe she had to be hospitalized for two weeks.

When we moved to Normal, eight years later, we were pregnant with our second son. The conventional medical wisdom was (and remains) that a prior C-section rules out a subsequent vaginal delivery. The stress of the contractions could cause the already once-breached uterus to rupture, with catastrophic consequences.

But we found a progressive obstetrician who was willing, with surgical suite at the ready, to give Diane a second if limited opportunity to dilate. In the end, that son was also delivered by C-section, but it was nothing like the exigent extraction of our first child. (I was present in the operating room to hold him, from the very moment he was born.)

We were fully ensconced in the community for our third son's birth, just 15 months later. By then, we had a midwife in the group, and Diane wanted to do what she had already watched several of her spiritual sisters do. When her time came, she would repair to our bedroom, surrounded by the midwife, our trance-medium and the women she felt closest to. Swapping war stories about their own deliveries, they would chat and laugh the hours away, while I passed the time in the living room, with my brothers and a keg.

But I was still a lawyer. I knew what it meant that at the first mention of the home-birth idea, every obstetrician we consulted refused even to participate in Diane's prenatal care. (Any appearance of acquiescing in a home-birth after not one but two C-sections was a malpractice suit waiting to happen.)

An anesthesiologist who had been in our couples group now became at once my caring friend and relentless tormentor. Almost to the day Diane went into labor, he harangued me with the gory details of a delivery he had attended where the woman's uterus did burst, resulting in her death.

Mr. Dillon, however, had given his spiritually informed consent to the home-birth idea. Unlike the obstetricians, his disincarnate status gave him *de facto* if not absolute (*karmic*) immunity for any bad result. So my "faith," along with all the assumptions and emotional investments that had brought us to this moment, was on a potentially deadly collision course with the remnants of my common sense.

Days before she went into labor, I begged Diane to re-consider. Weeping, I confessed my mortal dread: "If you or the baby dies, I will never forgive myself for letting this insanity go forward." But in the face of my panic, Diane showed unwavering confidence—in Dillon, in her own body and in the home-birth plan.

As did our third son, who soon sailed smoothly down her vaginal canal, right up into my outstretched arms.

16

Final Straws

The above "miracle" probably extended our stay in the community by another year. But our continuing financial irresponsibility and Sherman and Tanya's increasingly authoritarian leadership continued to up the ante.

The rabbis of the Talmud used to say, *"Im eyn kemach, eyn Torah* -- Without bread, there can *be* no spirituality." This is a lesson our community never grasped. Instead of all going out and getting full-time jobs, we lurched from one financial crisis to another. Our still intense, still important communal processes felt increasingly like they were taking place on the deck of the Titanic.

But the mid 1980's marked the run up to the savings and loan crisis, when, as in the case of the more recent housing bubble, our financial institutions couldn't give money away fast enough. So each time I became convinced our financial ship was finally going down, some new letter would arrive, informing me that in light of my "excellent payment history," my credit line was once again being *increased*. (And on each such occasion, I would wonder whether this was God, throwing me another lifeline, or Satan, luring me farther out to sea.)

Having come this far, I don't believe we would have left

the community based on our financial distress standing alone. But two other issues arose, in quick succession, that seemed to leave us no real choice.

The first was ideological. A senior member of the group announced, with Tanya and Sherman's apparent blessing, that he was leaving his wife. Her lagging spiritual progress was ostensibly preventing him from realizing his own fullest potential. So he was going to "put God and spiritual-purpose first"—even though Dillon himself had pronounced this couple "eternal soulmates."

And on that point everything else now seemed to teeter. This wasn't the first of our couples to have gone their separate ways. But those previous cases had posed no real challenge to the eternal soulmate construct. Their separations had simply provided the proof in the pudding that the parting spouses *had not been* eternal soulmates in the first place.

This was both the paradox and the genius of the eternal soulmate theory. So long as the couple stayed together, its eternal status was never questioned. In exchange, the community expected both individuals to *act* like eternal soulmates (according to our strict behavioral and energetic standards). Which, in turn, put their marital staying-power constantly to the test. We thus drove our individual and relational processes at full-throttle, for as long as we (or they) could keep from throwing a rod.

But *this* clever fellow had extracted from Dillon a cosmic guarantee: that he and his wife *were* eternal soulmates; and thus, implicitly, that his love for her *would* stand the test of time. (As if being dead made Dillon that smart.)

Did I say this problem was *ideological?* The demise of

this relationship threatened much more than our psycho-spiritual theory in the abstract. For had we not predicated our own, born-again couplehood on *its* spiritual provenance, as similarly vouched for by Dillon? Had we overlooked, at the time, some spiritual fine print that made this just a *limited* eternal warranty?

When invited to address this alarming development, Dillon's own mood turned uncharacteristically grave. "Such inability of soulmates to progress together is exceedingly rare," he stammered. But his spiritual affect was unmistakably shamefaced. He didn't have to say, "Pay no attention to that little man standing behind the curtain!" The annulment of this outlier of an aberrant, underperforming, eternal-in-name-only ("spiritual-style") union said it for him.

Did I also speculate moments ago that economic considerations *standing alone* would not have driven us from the community? This facile revisionism cast our wobbly financial status into newly exigent doubt. For if a senior member of the group could so summarily dump his own vouchsafed soulmate, what must that say about the commitment he had only derivatively made to me and mine?

But the final straw was a confrontation between Sherman and me over the nature and extent of his own spiritual authority. As a follow-up to the couples counseling Diane and I had done at Purdue, she was asked to teach a formal course there, in family dynamics. And this time, she invited not just me but Tanya and Sherman to team-teach the course with her.

True to our convictions, we tried to structure the course around the theme of honest communication. So I shouldn't have been surprised when, a month or two into the semester, one of the students took me aside and invited me to walk my talk. He asked me why Diane and I seemed to defer, so thoroughly and at every turn, to Tanya and Sherman. "They appear to be *controlling* you," the student boldly asserted.

It took a lot of guts for this young man to share such an observation with me. He knew nothing of our history with Tanya and Sherman and had no apparent ax to grind. "We defer out of respect for their insight and experience," I tentatively responded.

But when I recounted the above on the ride home from class, Sherman's reaction all but made the student's case. "You betrayed me," he declared, with little affect and even less circumspection. "You should have acknowledged me forthrightly as your spiritual teacher. And told the student that as such, it was *fine* with you to be controlled by me."

We rode the rest of the way home in stunned silence. I waited a few days for the dust to settle, hoping Sherman would get in touch with just how out of control his ego had become. Instead the standoff escalated. The family that had been sharing our home abruptly gathered up their belongings and moved out. This without benefit of five minutes' process, though we had endured countless hours of tortured soul-searching with them over the most trifling issues of daily life.

The man who had quit his night job at the post office with my blessing now refused to let his little daughter *play* with our toddler son. A woman who had been nursemaid and aunt to our infant retrieved her coffeemaker and dishrag from our house. And never held our baby again.

The weeks and months that followed were the bitterest

of our lives. I've weighed long and hard my gains, losses, choices and responsibility for all I experienced in the community. Whether I could have learned what I learned there at less personal cost, I cannot say.

I know only that the above incident shattered my illusion of accountability with this group of people. And that any further growth there would have been vastly overpriced.

PART THREE

WORKING
WITHOUT A NET

17

Two Little Pigs

Looking back on this difficult time, I believe my greatest challenge was to separate the wheat from the chaff of the preceding three years. But our first priority was to re-establish diplomatic relations with our "blood" families, if they would have us back. And I would have to explain myself to Jack Murphy, in the hope I still had a full-time job to return to.

While packing up for our move back to the City, I came across some correspondence to my older brother, summarizing what I had *thought* we were doing in Normal:

Dear Fred,

One of the things I so admire about Murphy and Green is their open-mindedness about the lifestyle we've opted for. The day I told Murphy I wanted to go part-time, he held his calls for 20 minutes to hear all about our decision to move to Normal and the spiritual community we are forging here. I told him about Mr. Dillon and the influence he's had on our marriage and values. Then I steeled myself for a skeptical if not outright disparaging response.

After hearing me out, Murphy squared himself in

his seat, locking me eyeball to eyeball. "You know, Elliot, if you had told me all this shit the first day you walked into this office . . . " Jack paused here to spit a mouthful of tobacco into the cup he kept on his desk for that special purpose, and I clutched the sides of my chair, waiting for the other shoe to drop . . . "We'd still be sitting here having this conversation."

*I appreciated Murphy's gesture and regretted not having been more candid with him about our life and values long before that day. So now, with somewhat similar trepidation, I want to let you, my brother, in on "the **rest** of our story":*

*Diane and I moved to Normal (1) to work on our relationship, which, after twelve years, was hanging by a thread. We hoped to make a fresh start, this time putting the marriage ahead of everything else; (2) to learn to **be** more authentic, first and foremost with each other. That meant getting a handle on neurotic behaviors, the unconscious as well as the conscious, that have dominated our communication for most of our married life; (3) to enhance our self-awareness (bringing the unconscious **into** consciousness), by trusting our feelings the way we've previously trusted only thoughts and opinions. (From this perspective, I have learned that the heart has more to offer than the mind and that loving trumps "telling it like it is."); (4) to share our personal and relational process with others who are similarly committed, thereby creating an extended family environment for ourselves and our children; (5) to share, also, our material things, in the hope of outgrowing our selfishness; (6) to overcome petty ego, trading the illusion of gross control for a* *subtler, less provincial sense of purpose. In short: (7) to put more faith in God, realizing that our success only **seems** to spring from credentials, worry, manipulation and being in the right place at the right time.*

I anticipate some brotherly concern as you cogitate on the above. But the simple truth is, we believe in God. And while that in itself is hardly news, our goal here is to keep our daily business so informed; to draw, from every task and interaction, some small sip of spiritual content. For that is how we express and nourish our nascent faith.

Fred, I've been afraid to share such aspirations with you in the past. Part of my process here seems a weaning from whatever has so deterred me. I guess I just haven't wanted to hear you accuse me of being "in need of professional help."

Which of the above tenets would I still claim, from the carnage of our failed utopian experiment? I found and reread Fred's letter answering the above:

Elliot,

There's a difference between being open-minded and empty-headed. I think your current lifestyle follows the pattern you established earlier of chasing after false gods and relying on phony "support" groups for "love and guidance." Sorry, but I believe problems related to self-image/self-respect are best dealt with in a one-to-one relationship with a competent psychiatrist.

This is not an "accusation"; it's loving, caring, sound counsel. Healthy individuals don't need nor desire to "share" such intimacies as you describe with groups. People—healthy, emotionally mature people—establish appropriate boundaries.

I'm struck by the vague psychobabble that threads its way through your letter, e.g., the "illusion of control" and "the heart has more to offer than the mind." Your dogma is of course anti-reason precisely because it is unreasonable!

*But of your seven tenets, the last two concern me the most; because you, my brother, aren't "overcoming" ego, you're **wallowing** in it; and because healthy people don't give over their control—not to gurus, ghosts, groups or gods, not to **anyone**, not **ever!** It's when we abandon our own reason and are content to rely on external authority that trouble begins.*

I share these feelings with you because I care about you and want to see you grow up already and take charge of your own life. Bertrand Russell wrote:

> *There is something feeble and a little contemptible about a man who cannot face the perils of life without the help of comfortable myths. Almost inevitably, some part of him is aware that they are myths and that he believes them only because they are comforting. But he dare not face this thought! Moreover, since he is aware, however dimly, that his opinions are not rational, he becomes furious when they are disputed.*

*Elliot, you are so intelligent, articulate and gifted. Get some **real** help for the emotional needs. As they say around here, "Wake up and smell the coffee!" And spare me the spiritual sloganeering; don't en-*

gage me in polemics. I can't validate your mishoo-gas![13]

Love,
Your brother, Fred

A quarter century later, I see both the love and the wisdom in my brother's message (even as he keeps a wary eye out, to this day, for further flare-ups of my *mishoogas*). My reply at the time, however, was just as Bertrand Russell had predicted:

Dear Fred,

*I'll try to keep my polemics to a minimum. The difference between us is that you view belief in God as unreasonable, immature and a symptom of mental illness. If there is a God, what could possibly be unhealthy about wanting to subordinate one's personal will to His? On the other hand, what is so admirable, responsible and healthy about "establishing appropriate boundaries" (with everyone **but** the recommended psychiatrist)?*

You sing the praises of psychiatry, to which you've never subjected yourself, while condemning the spirit (likewise without benefit of personal experience). If that is not the height of presumptuousness, I am definitely wallowing in something.

Your brother, Elliot

*P. S. **Fuck** Bertrand Russell.*

Having long since obtained the recommended one-on-one with a psychiatrist (Chapter 22, *infra*), I am fairly con-

---

[13] Yiddish for nonsense (craziness).

fident the good doctor would today give me a decent bill of mental health. (Who knows, of course, what Bertrand Russell might say.) But in 1986, when I had to call on Fred for financial help to get me and my family back up on our feet, I felt like the little pig who had built with sticks, coming hat-in-hand to the one who had built with bricks.

Some part of me dimly sensed that I had laid some solid, if half-baked bricks of my own. But for the present, they were affording my family and me no shelter and little comfort.

18

Returning to the Fold

Needless to say, we were anxious to do whatever we could to ease this transition for our children. The obvious first step was to join a synagogue, where they would be reintroduced to our religious traditions and hopefully, find a whole new set of friends.

The nearest congregation was a small, Conservative one that had just hired its first female rabbi. She proved as welcoming to us as the congregation would prove to her (and nonjudgmental about our recent spiritual digression). So by the time of our eldest son's bar mitzvah, three years later, he was well prepared, and we were reintegrated, as a family, into the Jewish community.

A few more years had passed when a friend mentioned that her synagogue was in a crisis. Their cantor had left, and the High Holidays were just around the corner. Did I happen to know of anyone who might be able to fill in?

Only months before, quite fortuitously, I had started taking *voice* lessons again! And this time, apparently, I did improve. Perhaps the long hiatus had allowed my voice to finally finish changing, my throat chakra to open or some anatomically unrelated karma to clear. However it happened, I soon found myself leading a 900-family congregation in prayer.

For the next six years, what was supposed to have been a one-time, High-Holiday appointment turned into every Saturday morning, holiday services, adult and children's choir rehearsals and the occasional wedding or funeral. And though I've long since given up those nearly full-time cantorial responsibilities, I have continued to serve as a High Holiday cantor, at one synagogue or another, almost every year for the last two decades. It is a role in which I feel blessed and privileged to serve.

But is it presumptuous of me to stand before God as a *shaliach tzibur* (community spokesperson), having personally veered so substantially from the prescribed Jewish-religious path? I will leave that judgment to others, except to note that I have never concealed my history as a wandering Jew from the rabbis with whom I have worked—or anyone else for that matter.

But there was one interesting incident, early in my tenure at that 900-family synagogue. It was the bat-mitzvah of a girl whose parents were pillars of the congregation. Looking down from the dais to where the family was seated, I spotted someone who had lived in the *ashram* during my days as a follower of Gurudeva Ji.

After the service, we greeted each other and I learned that he was *still* a follower of the guru. But before I got to hear more about that, the father of the bat mitzvah girl came rushing over, alarm written all over his face.

Now I may of course have been projecting. But my old friend and I both knew the source of the proud papa's angst. The very last thing he wanted, on this special family occasion, was for his own, unchaperoned younger brother to be sharing any of *his mishoogas* . . . and with the *Cantor,* of all people!

So, accepting our karma, we smiled and shook hands. And with a respectful, if strategic nod to the fast closing elder brother, I moved on to greet the next group of congregants.

19

Meanwhile, Back at the Day-Job

When I first limped back into Jack Murphy's office, on the heels of our exit from the community, I was relieved to find his door still open to me. So at the firm over the next few years, I kept my nose to the grindstone, trying to re-assure my employers I still had what it took, professionally. I outlasted the jibes about searching for "higher authorities" and resumed the persona of the scholarly if eccentric legal analyst and writer. I got good results on some complex cases, published an article in the Loyola Law Journal and stood poised to reclaim my professional *bona fides*.

But some part of me, unrepentant of my past and still uncertain of my worldly direction, found it difficult to confine myself to the straight and narrow of law firm life. I was frankly frustrated by the limited occasion it was affording me for meaningful interaction with other human beings.

This may come as a surprise to anyone whose image of lawyers derives from some televised courtroom drama. The fact is, even "litigators" spend most of their time sequestered at their desks, poring over documents of one sort or another. There are scores of these solitary hours for each one spent in the lively cross-examination of a witness.

In addition, most lawyers tend toward emotional reticence. It is, after all, our discretion (and our *un*emotional aura of authority) that commend us to our clients. Nevertheless, while I hardly expected the kind of self-revealing processes that had been the staple of my interactive diet in the community, the sterility of what passes for communication among lawyers was the other end of the interpersonal spectrum.

The time came for me to be considered for partnership. This is, in law firm culture, what tenure is in academia. Partnership would thus place the firm's and, by extension, the legal community's imprimatur on my professional achievements. Given the slow if scenic career path I had taken, I craved the recognition and sense of identity that "making partner" would finally afford me.

But my dissatisfaction with the interpersonal pedestrianism of law practice (and perhaps my inability to let things go too smoothly for too long) got the better of me. So it occurred to me I might be happier in the role of a judge than I had been as an attorney.

It also happened, just at that time, that there were an unusual number of openings on the Cook County Circuit Court. I had some political contacts in the Governor's office, where those appointments would be made. But the current Governor was also nearing the end of his term.

This put me in a kind of "catch 22" situation. To be a viable judicial candidate, I would need the strong backing of my current employers, Jack Murphy and Jack Green. But this was hardly the time to be discussing with them my desire to be working somewhere else. If such candor were to cost me my partnership, it might dash, at the same stroke, any prospect I had for appointment to the bench.

As I ruminated on this dilemma, it struck me that this was the same moment (another layer of the onion) I had faced when applying for the job at Murphy & Green in the first place. Would I share any more of myself with them now than I had then? Or would I be hearing Jack Murphy say, down the road, "Of course we'll support you for judge; but had you told us two years ago that you aspired to the bench, we would gladly have supported you then."?

Thus determined to practice what I had preached in the letter to my brother Fred, I concluded that making partner was of little value if it required me to stifle my legitimate conflicts and ambitions. So I requested a meeting with Jack Murphy, Jack Green and the head of the firm's litigation section, Kevin O'Reilly.

They did in fact question my commitment to the firm in the light of my interest in the bench. But the discussion was fair, frank and healthy. Afterwards, I tried to capture the essence of our conversation in the following:

MEMORANDUM

TO: *JLM, JJG and KMO*

FROM: *ET*

DATE: *June 16, 1989*

RE: *Partnership and "Commitment"*

Just a few more thoughts about the meaning of partnership and the commitment to the firm that my judicial aspiration has apparently called into question. As a starting point, I think we can all agree that our present, employer-employee relationship has kept *plenty of food on our respective tables. Having tested each other to that extent, I see the partnership decision as now upping the ante for all of us, precisely by moving the discussion **beyond** the breadwinning per se.*

As an applicant for this enhanced status, what I'm about to say may be the height of presumptuousness. But the partnership I seek, far from a mere honorific, is also much more than the financial opportunity (and responsibility) the term legalistically implies. So when Jack M. says he needs partners "who will be there to share the load with him," the potential partner in me hears a deeper statement.

*"Financial commitment" is an oxymoron. We all have financial **obligations;** but I've always thought of the commitment between partners as something more personal: a heartfelt desire to work for the other's highest good, in the broadest sense and as an end in itself. To be sure, such an alliance should not come at any one partner's financial expense; but neither, in my view, need it compromise any partner's non-monetary aspirations.*

*People who are with you for economic advantage alone, however mutual, will be gone the moment their financial self-interest so dictates. So if Jack ever **is** left holding the bag, it will be because he had "partners" who were obligated to him financially but, when push came to shove, **not** personally committed.*

This isn't just semantics. I believe that loyalty is a function of relationship in a way that promises and even performance can never be. And that perspective has made promoting myself as the productive equal *or better) of this or that other candidate for partner-ship not just off-putting, but off-point. For while such zero-sum competitiveness may get you a good assort-ment of brilliant lawyers, trial lawyers, rainmakers and worker bees, in the end, it doesn't engender loy-alty. Once the rainmaker convinces **himself** just how good a rainmaker he really is, why should he stay here and make rain **for you?***

Jack G. was right. Our discussion was less about my desire to be a judge than my need to share these thoughts with you three. Relationship and prosperity aren't mutually exclusive, and I've got no bone to pick with financial security. (As Jack M. aptly put it, we wouldn't be beating our brains out together day in and day out if we were all rich instead of argumenta-tive.)

But just as you say you need partners who will be there for your bottom line, I need partners whose suc-cess cannot but grow with mine. What that means in this precise context is still a bit muddled for me, but perhaps the above will provide a backdrop for its fur-ther clarification.

I probably expended 30 non-billable hours on this effort to articulate, in the seemingly unreceptive environment of a busy law practice, ideals that had become part of me in the community. Kevin O'Reilley, who was valedictorian of his law school class, claimed not to understand a word of my memo. Nevertheless, he canceled a planned trip that would have absented him from the partners' meeting at which my fate was to be decided. And spearheaded the effort in my behalf.

I did simultaneously apply for the bench. But the commission that vets judicial candidates for the Governor could not get past my recent stint as a spiritual communist. The second time I applied, my interview seemed to go much smoother (the community never even came up).

"Yeah," Jack Murphy quipped when I still didn't make the cut. "They must have powwowed before you got there: 'Here comes the nut case . . . let's not *rile* him!'"

20

Process and Prosperity

My partnership memo and related conversations weren't the first time I had presumed to smuggle interpersonal process into the professional workings of Murphy & Green. When I first joined the firm, in 1983, three other recruits had come aboard at the same time. That being the case, Jack and Jack had left it to us to determine the order in which our names would appear on the letterhead.

Our foursome consisted of two recent graduates, one of whom had just finished clerking for the firm, a lawyer who had practiced for several years in another state and me, with more gray hair than all the other three combined. Someone suggested we draw straws and be done with this uncomfortable business. I pretended to be fine with that, but suggested we first take a few minutes, over lunch, to explore whether any of our names *should* come ahead of the others on the masthead.

At lunch, the woman who had clerked for the firm suggested such tenure might entitle her to seniority for letterhead purposes. The other recent grad countered that having himself clerked at one of Chicago's larger, more established firms, his decision to join the young upstarts, Murphy & Green, had astounded his peers; in response to which, he had assured them that in just a few years, his name would be right up near the *top* of an ever-growing M & G letterhead.

"Leapfrogging the three of you would get me off to a fabulous start!" he now enthused. Then, in a more pensive tone, he added, "And it would impress the *hell* out of my father."

The lawyer who had practiced in another state was also surprisingly candid. He wasn't too concerned about a couple of rungs, up or down, on the masthead. But he made a point of admonishing us that so conciliatory a stance—*were it to leave the room*—might tarnish his reputation as a hard-nosed litigator.

Touched by all this self-disclosure (and realizing the lunch hour was almost over), I suggested my name come last; and that the others quickly reach a consensus as to the proper order for theirs. Pandemonium ensued. You would have thought I had pulled out a revolver and pointed it at my temple! It became a matter of utmost urgency to talk me out of this, lest the others be perceived as having taken unfair *advantage* of me.

In the face of this uproar, I offered to break the logjam by going *first* on the letterhead. We all had a good laugh and then proceeded to draw straws.

The meeting thus concluded with the same result and yet a totally different feeling than if we had just drawn straws in the first place. I don't remember the order in which our names ended up. Within a few years, I was the only one of the four still *on* the letterhead (which by then, in all events, was alphabetical). But I do know no one left that meeting feeling shortchanged by the outcome.

Looking back on these, my prime breadwinning years, it

occurs to me that "climbing the letterhead" meant no more (and no less) than squaring my lofty pronouncements with my own productivity, on a sustainable basis. When all is said and done, that's what walking one's talk means in the business and professional world.

And what of those whose economic fate was also riding on my effort to integrate what I had learned in the community with my professional and worldly responsibilities? In those years, I made them my safety net. Before embarking on any course that threatened to impact us financially, I'd convene a family meeting. There I'd lay out all the risks, like the hospital does when you go in for surgery. I'd ask my kids what they thought I should do . . . and whether they were willing to absorb their share of the economic blow if things turned out badly.

In that sense, the caption on my partnership memo might just as well have read:

TO: JLM, JJG and KMO
FROM: ET, his WIFE and his BOYS

21

Worrying Wisely

"Worry is the worst murderer of mankind," Mr. Dillon used to declare. Pop-psychology and New-Age culture likewise tend to demonize stress, implying that the more we worry, the sicker we become (until eventually, we *die* of something). But Dillon was also fond of reminding us that "there *is* no death and there *are* no dead." In that case, what's the harm of a little worry now and then, especially if it gets us in gear to accomplish something in our physical interim?

Over the years at Murphy & Green, I conducted an orientation session for our new lawyers. The challenge was to give the fresh troops a realistic sense of the focus and productivity a successful practice demanded—if possible, without greatly exacerbating the first-job, survival-mentality that already had them quaking in their boots. But one point I felt obliged to get across at these sessions was that every file in the office came with its own, case-specific quotient of worries.

The discussion went something like this:

You may think the people at the top of the hierarchy have all the worries, but it's really the other way around. If there's a file I've not found time to get to, my worry meter starts buzzing every time I glance in its direction. But the second I hand that file off to you, the worry, like so much toxic radon emanating from the earth below, migrates from my office *into yours*.

Now you'll be getting assignments from a number of partners, none of whom will be losing much sleep over how you're reconciling their competing demands on your time. So it will be your responsibility to deal with both the sensational and the relational implications of the resultant stress. In other words, you must *feel* (stay conscious of) the pressure. In large measure, it's what keeps us on top of what we're being paid to stay on top of. But you must also remain conscious of your own needs and limitations. That means monitoring the impact, both here and in your larger context, of all we're demanding of you.

That too is part of good lawyering. And it can be a fine line between impressing us with your uncomplaining industry and having the good sense to say, "I just can't *do* all that you're asking of me."

After that, I'd try to lighten things up by telling them of the time, years before, that Jack Murphy had asked how *I* was coming on a particular assignment. "I've still got two projects ahead of yours," I answered, blithely turning to leave the room. Jack stopped me in my tracks. "Uh, Elliot," he asked awkwardly but pointedly, "who's *worrying* about that file, you or *me?*"

"I'll tell you what," I shot back. "It's going to take me a week and a half to get to that file. If you want me to worry about it in the meantime, I can do that. But it's also fine with me if *you* want to do the worrying."

Caught off guard by my *chutzpah,* Jack gave a confused

shrug and let me get on about my more pressing business.

Now few other associates would have risked such impudence with the senior partner of the firm. But this was during my community days, when I was buoyed by a false sense of spiritual security. When the shit eventually hit the fan, I had to come to grips, once again, with the dilemma facing every other mortal being: Which files are mine, which are Jack Murphy's and which are *God's?* How *much* worrying should I be doing, about what . . . and in what order?

I thus found myself relating to Murphy quite differently when he summoned me, not too many years later, for a meeting with an important client. At that time, our growing firm was housed in two separate buildings, about a block apart. So I grabbed my briefcase and started jogging from my office over to Jack's.

Halfway there, I was struck by my unseemly sense of urgency. "You're a 'grown attorney,'" I remarked to myself. "Why so nervous about a meeting with 'the boss' and his 'important client'?" Except that I was out of breath, the meeting proved routine, resulting in the transfer to me of a box of documents relevant to a potential lawsuit. I set the box on the rear seat of my car, intending to peruse the material at home, over the weekend.

A day or so later, I got a frantic call from Diane. "Something terrible has happened," she began. "I was driving on the parkway and the door of the car just *flew open!"* Picturing one of my kids flying out, I was relieved to learn the box of documents was the only casualty. "Your papers," Diane somberly reported, "are all over the Expressway."

Now these were original files, reflecting a 10-year history of transactions between the parties to the prospective litigation. They were irreplaceable. I couldn't imagine how I was going to break this news to Jack Murphy, especially after the fuss he (and I) had seemed to be making to impress this particular client.

With no pressing deadline in the case, I thought I'd wait for some inspiration (or some bus) to strike me. But I didn't get to wait long. The very next day, Jack called to say the client was back with some further thoughts he wanted to share with us about the case. This time, it was a long, slow walk from my office over to Jack's.

"You owe me 100 bucks," Jack said as I entered the room. "A hundred bucks?" I restated. "Did we have a bet about something?"

"No," Jack drawled, "a hundred bucks is what I just handed Richard here. He gave his own $100 to some *fireman* . . . who showed up at his *house* this morning . . . WITH THAT BOX OF DOCUMENTS **WE GAVE YOU THE OTHER DAY!**"

In a hot tub some years later, Jack and I were reminiscing about this incident. I reminded him of a certain imperiousness with which he had summoned me to that initial client meeting, like some smart nerd he kept on the payroll for just such occasions. "If you need to show off for your clients like that, I'm willing to play the part for you from time to time," I assured him. "I just can't predict what outside forces might intervene to sabotage *both* our expectations!"

"And what *you* need to know," Jack responded affectionately, "is that I'm willing to do the same for you whenever you need me to." That's when I knew I really had "made partner."

Jack gave me one other gift that night. He thanked me for a conversation many years before. "You know the one I mean," he said wistfully. "Over lunch that day . . . in the *Chinese restaurant.*" (See p.93.)

22

Pills and Process

Some time in the early '90s, my brother Earl went through a personal crisis. I found myself advising him, as our elder brother had counseled me, to see a psychiatrist. But in recommending the very one-on-one professional relationship I myself had rejected, I was reminded of a story I had heard at *satsang*.

A woman was at wits end with her young son, who only wanted to eat sweets. Her guru suggested she bring the boy to him; but not for two weeks. At the appointed time, the child was so moved by the guru's words, he promptly cut his candy intake by half.

Years later, the woman reminded the guru of the impact he had had on her now grown (and healthy) son. "But I've always wondered, Master, why you made me wait the two weeks before bringing the boy to see you."

"When you first mentioned your son to me," the guru answered, "my own sweet tooth was out of control. I needed time to clean up *my* eating habits before I could presume to speak to your son about his!"

It was thus my younger brother's distress, rather than my elder's cajoling, that led me gently but firmly to my decision. I simply couldn't help but notice how similar my own eating habits were to Earl's.

It seems almost comical, looking back, that after a guru, a ghost and all the accompanying *mishoogas,* it took a simple look in the mirror of my younger brother's eyes to recognize and accept my clinical predicament. And begin clicking the heels of my own ruby slippers.

I walk a fine line in so describing my decision to "get help" of this more mainstream sort. I've not arrived at Chapter 22 only to recant the psychospiritual convictions I've gone to such lengths to relate above. The fact is, I don't see any contradiction between them and the more conventional course I was now set upon. For had I established the "appropriate one-to-one relationship" 20 years earlier, I might well be a different person today, but not necessarily a better, happier or wiser one. (And what kind of movie would it have been had Dorothy clicked her heels three times before ever meeting the Tin Man or dealing with the Wicked Witch of the West?)

I had met Dr. Blumenthal some years before. In the aftermath of our break with Tanya and Sherman, I had reported to the Jewish Family Service for an assessment of my emotional state. After a few sessions, the social worker assigned to my case called Blumenthal in, to see if he thought I should be on medication.

But I had come to that session directly from a deposition. After observing 30 seconds of my upbeat, adrenaline-boosted demeanor, Blumenthal pronounced me "not-depressed" and left the room. End of consultation.

I did not hold that against him when I was finally ready to get into ongoing treatment. So for the next couple of years, we took a more in-depth look at those parallel personas, spiritual and worldly, that Sarah had so long ago helped me identify. And my chronic inability to find satisfaction, for very long, on *either* track.

Through this therapy, I came to understand that my spiritual leanings were symbolically but perniciously linked to my mother, the nurturer; while my ambitious side was staunchly associated with my father, the provider. But Dad's providence came at a Faustian price: Nightly, he raved that the *greenback* was God (and peace of mind, the *rich* man's booty). So setting no store in his affection, I vowed to earn some scant respect. Someday, somehow, I would "show him the money."

Mother, not surprisingly, was Father's better half. Like TV's Mr. Rogers, she loved us just the way we were. "Life is what you make it," she chirped, "so do what makes you *happy*." She was there for us at school events our father never came to. Still, I heard his muffled groan beneath the weight of her good cheer.

But then, as I moved from adolescence into adulthood, Mother's focus took an inexplicable turn. She stopped inquiring about my vocal or religious pursuits and now began each conversation by asking how things were going for me *at work*. For some reason, this always felt like a punch in the stomach.

Blumenthal helped me see that I experienced such inquiries as a betrayal of the spiritual alliance I thought Mother and I had forged. As it turned out, her values were much closer to Dad's than I had ever imagined. And it was a slippery slope from there to an even more devastating realization: that the two were no less aligned in his nightly atrocities.

So long as my psyche had Mother pegged as "good" and Dad as "bad," I was as stuck as they were in their relational homeostasis. And it was this subconscious polarity that was keeping the values and aspirations associated with each parent at cross-purposes—just as Larry and Ruth had always seemed to be. I thus lived in a state of chronic ambivalence, siding mostly with Mother's more "spiritual" outlook, but always with a cache of loyalty to Dad's more cynical worldview.

Important as the above insights were for me, my "quality of life" was impacted less by them than by Prozac. This time, Blumenthal prescribed it for me at the very start of treatment. But it was only some ten or twelve weeks later that I experienced a remarkable and rather sudden shift in my emotional sensation. I use that phrase to convey that the improvement seemed to have nothing to do with my relationships *per se,* or how I was conducting them.

Simply put, I felt well. Not the exhilaration that accompanied a victory in court; nor the "blissed-out" state at the feet of the guru. This was an unvarnished sense of well-being, unrelated to any notion of earning *or* grace. It was like coming into an emotional nest egg; one that had been accruing interest all those years it had gone unclaimed.

The transformation was all the more astonishing for the fact that in the three months it took the Prozac to kick in, I hadn't been in any acute distress. It was as if someone had just flipped a switch . . . and every positive thing in my life was suddenly shouting, "SURPRISE!"

My ardent inner process seemed abruptly obsolete. Yet in my daily interactions, my energy was uncharacteristically robust. I was fully engaged. *Unconflicted.*

"What are you *on?*" Sarah asked in a mildly accusatory tone. I had just entered the foyer of her house, not having seen her for over a year. I didn't tell her right away it was Prozac she was sensing in my aura, though I had brought the bottle of pills along with me to the session. Indeed, I had scheduled this appointment precisely to get Sarah's take on how this medication was affecting me. (I certainly knew I was feeling better, but still wanted her unique kind of second opinion.)

Sarah, I should mention, is an organic health nut. Her idea of getting the day off to a good start is a glass of fresh-squeezed carrot juice. She avoids not just medications, but microwave ovens. Nevertheless, after tuning in to these pills in my system, she conceded they were doing me some good. Then she added, almost grudgingly, "You won't always *need* this medication."

I have my own misgivings about relying on a synthetic chemical to feel well. But certain sequelae of my karma are still eluding total cure. I remain open to a more organic healing, with the fullest self-awareness and relational integrity of which I'm presently capable. Even as I get by, until then, with a little help from my pharmaceutical friend.

23

Insight vs. Healing

There was one aspect of my depression that stood apart from the more endogenous illness. As the extended family assembled each year at my sister's house, for Thanksgiving, I would sink into a lethargic state that would last the entire weekend. In particular, it was my Mother's physical presence that seemed to bring on this distinct emotional fog.

In the spring of 1989, I was greeting relatives who had flown in for my first son's Bar Mitzvah. When I spotted my mother down a long airport concourse, the degree and suddenness of my emotional shift was startling. I plunged from a state of anticipation and high energy into one of lethargy and depression.

Sarah had also come in for the Bar Mitzvah, so at the first opportunity, I asked if she could shed any light on what had just happened. She said only that it had to do with some traumatic incident, when I was 10 or 11.

Out of the blue several years later, Mother invited me to unburden myself of any criticism I might have of her parenting. This was shortly after my father had died, and I suspect it had to do with some grief counseling she was getting. (She mentioned that she was making the same energy-clearing overture to each of her four children.)

We were sitting under a large elm tree in the front yard when Mother thus propositioned me. Ironically, I had been keeping our interactions to a minimum that visit, trying to ward off the kind of tailspin described above. Now she was asking me not just to stop the warding off but to immerse myself in the very energy that had come between us.

An incident sprang to mind—probably what Sarah was alluding to above, though it occurred around the time of my own Bar Mitzvah (age 13, not 10 or 11). Mother had left the house after a heavier than usual course of verbal battering by my father. But instead of drifting off into his usual sleepy stupor, Dad went straight to the phone.

"Hello, June? This is *Bob Schaeffer.* I'd like to see you tonight." He then took a shower, got dressed to kill and left the house for the rest of the evening.

For the next few days, I was caught up in a crisis of conscience and divided loyalty. Should I rat out my dad to my mother? Since she seemed the innocent victim of both his nightly abuse and this singular betrayal, I decided she deserved my allegiance.

Without batting an eye, Mother told me I was *mistaken* in what I had heard. She actually managed a chuckle over my "misinterpretation." A friend of hers, *Joan,* was training to be a manicurist and had been doing Dad's *nails,* for practice. Undoubtedly, it was Joan (not "June") he had called for this spur of the moment appointment.

"As for 'Bob Schaeffer,'" Mother continued, "that was just a stage name Dad used during his acting days at the Pittsburgh Playhouse" (with which "Joan," presumably, was familiar).

That night, I heard my parents yelling at each other from behind their bedroom door. Only now do I realize how different—how much *healthier* this shouting match was than the nightly bombardments to which we had all inured ourselves. How much more overt . . . and to the point.

At the time though, I felt guilty that I had precipitated a worsening of my parents' status quo (disruption of their relational homeostasis, as I would now call it). My father was especially distant toward me in the aftermath of the first real fight he'd had with my mother in many years.

Some days later, I was riding in the car with my parents. My instinct even then was to take initiative in the face of their communicative default. So from my position in the back seat, I searched for a way to break the ice about all this.

At age 13, I didn't know how to just say, "Mom and Dad, I've been worrying about your situation, scared the two of you might get divorced; and upset over being left completely in the dark about whatever is going on between you." So instead, I said, "Dad, tell me about your days at the Pittsburgh Playhouse."

"DON'T TALK ABOUT THAT!" my dad barked at me. For the rest of the ride, not another word was spoken. For the next *28 years,* nothing further would be said.

As I now pondered my mother's unexpected invitation to address any emotional grievance I might have, the memory of these events flooded my consciousness. After reminding her of the incident, I took a deep breath and said:

Mother, do you see how you left me out on a limb after I had allied myself with you in this drama? We might have taken some comfort in our shared (if quite different) aggrievement. Instead, you lied to me. Then you "gave me up to the enemy." And even after you and Dad had fought it out, you never came back to clean things up on my end; or even to reassure me that the two of you were trying to turn things around.

This was no diatribe against my mother. My words were soft and tearful. She also cried, and after only a bit of defending, took responsibility for what had occurred between us so many years before.

From that day forward, I never suffered another depressive meltdown on coming into my mother's physical presence. That specific energy was dissipated by our belated, but heartfelt communication.

I assume that my remaining, more endogenous depression no less has its antecedents in specific (if cumulative) interpersonal experiences. Or in current relational circumstances, the full implications of which I have not yet been ready to address. Just as medical research sifts for clues within a cancer cluster, so it behooves us to monitor our emotional fluctuations, to ferret out any linkage between our interactions and their psychosomatic effects. That is largely what psychotherapy attempts to do.

The healing with my mother also reminded me that identifying our emotional wounds and healing them are two different things. Sarah had helped me connect the Bob Schaeffer incident with my longstanding emotional allergy to Mother. But that suspicion of cause and effect had afforded me no relief from the symptomatology.

In this sense, intellectual and emotional awareness are like twins, separated at birth, each vaguely sensing their incompleteness. True objectivity, the kind that presages our emotional healing, entails both seeing and feeling our inter-personal reality, at the selfsame instant.

This experience with my mother also taught me that as long as I breathe air (and so long as those with whom I may yet effect some emotional and relational healing continue to breathe), I must take my opportunities to resolve things with those who have hurt me (and with those whom I have hurt). I was attempting to do that, however clumsily, when I asked my dad to tell me more about "Bob Schaeffer." It just took me another 28 years to come up with a more artful approach. And for my mother, at least, to make herself a little vulnerable.

24

A Matter of Apples and Eggs

But how do we heal relationships with people who have died? Or who simply are not open to process, however gentle and well meaning?

My father now fell into both categories. He had certainly never invited feedback about his parenting. In fact, on the one occasion I attempted such a communication, he called me "holier than thou"; then dispatched me with his most caustic benediction: "Just remember," he sneered, *"the apple never falls far from the tree."*

I was revisiting that interaction some years later, during my morning commute. I had vowed that *this* little apple would move as far from the tree (and as fast) as it could thrust itself. "But how exactly *does* an apple 'thrust' itself?" I pondered while negotiating the morning rush hour.

I had recently read *The Road Less Traveled,* by M. Scott Peck, and for no particular reason, it occurred to me that my answer had something to do with *Peck;* that if I would poke around a little with this hint, the solution would soon present itself.

This kind of internal chitchat had become a habit for me by now, a harbinger of insight, encouraging me just to stay with the subject matter at hand, but in a relaxed sort of mental soft-focus. So I meditated on the unlikely mantra I'd been given: "Poke, poke; Peck, Peck; poke, poke; Peck Peck" . . . until the light came on:

You're not an apple, you're a *chicken!* . . . No, hold on . . . it's an *unborn CHICK,* growing ever more confined in its neurotic *egg.* From *inside* that egg, you can "thrust" with all your might, this way and that, but as your father aptly stated, you will only *roll* yourself so far.

Yet if, instead of thrusting, the chick just does what comes naturally—*pokes* and *PECKS* against the shell of that egg—it will, in due course, *HATCH.* And on that day (*bayom hahu*), discover things the apple can never know . . . like *FEET* (not to mention *WINGS!*).

I was so enamored of this "breakthrough," I called Diane just as soon as I got to work. "You are not going to *believe* what I am staring at," she said after hearing my story. As I was dialing her up from the office, my wife had been flipping through the pages of a magazine. And when the ringing of the phone interrupted her flipping, *this* is what her gaze had just fallen upon:

This portrait of me appeared in the November 19, 1990 issue of *Newsweek Magazine,* as part of an advertisement. (It is reprinted here with the permission of Alaska Airlines.)

PART FOUR

INTEGRATION

25

Community (According to M. Scott Peck)

The Road Less Traveled was one of those rare gifts that have inspired millions of people. It had a profound impact on me and as I read it, I felt a strong desire to meet the author. Little did I know that a few years later, I would be telling the above story at Peck's 60th birthday party—and presenting him with a framed copy of the chicken-picture, as a token of my appreciation.

I first met Peck after reading *The Different Drum; Community-Making and Peace.* In that book, he attempts to distill the psychological and communicative elements that have allowed encounter groups to reach a collective, psychosensory state he calls "community." When a speaking tour brought him to Chicago, I got to talk with Peck about this.

I asked him whether positing community as a process-induced, group sensation didn't reduce it to a peak experience, as opposed to something that might be sustained and integrated into normal life. He invited me to follow up with him on the issue, and in a subsequent letter, I confessed I'd had my fill of such collective peak moments. "Of what value are these weekend workshops," I challenged, "if none of us is willing or capable of achieving what you call 'community' in our ongoing contexts? And should we not be suspicious when our communicative zeal expresses itself not in the personal conundra of everyday life, but in contrived encounters with people we don't know and with whom we have no future?"

Peck wrote back and invited me to attend a workshop sponsored by his Foundation for Community Encouragement (FCE). So much for having had my fill of collective peak moments. I soon found myself seated in a circle of about 25 five people, in Knoxville, Tennessee.

From *The Different Drum,* I had a rough idea what was in store. In the first stage of community-building, the participants display the kind of sociable, performance-behavior I've described on page 84. (Everyone acts as if they are already *in* the desired community state.) Peck calls this phase of the process "Pseudocommunity."

In stage two ("Chaos"), the phoniness begins to break down. Somebody becomes impatient or otherwise confrontational, and things turn ugly.

By stage three, the participants start owning up to the fact that they really have no idea what "community" is or how to snap themselves into it. Peck calls this "Emptying." Someone finds the courage to test the waters of personal vulnerability, to communicate without pretense or manipulative agenda. And this, like a drop of water on a parched plant, somehow allows everyone else in the group to lower their own defenses.

The final stage, "Community," is that rare state of affinity or heightened group sensitivity that makes it safe for the participants to stop performing for and judging one another. It is a collective gestalt in which each person's unique presence, rather than his ideas or personality, is truly felt and unconditionally accepted.

Thus apprised of the community-building sequence, I came to the FCE weekend determined not to play the stage-two provocateur. But I was unable to restrain myself when a woman named Cindy, a veteran of previous FCE events, began describing the lengths to which she had gone, over her husband's protest, to get to this workshop. Confessing her need now to obtain the community fix she had purchased at so dear a price, she implored us to get on with the process, to move beyond the insincere banter of Pseudocommunity in which we were mired. "We have only three more hours," she somberly intoned, "to *make it* . . . into *real community.*"

"I DON'T GIVE A SHIT IF WE EVER GET TO SO-CALLED 'COMMUNITY'!" I heard myself erupting. "If you haven't achieved it in all the time you've had with your own husband, what good is this fleeting and artificial state you want us to induce here at his further expense?"

So much for "Pseudocommunity." Cindy came back at me with both barrels blazing:

"YOU SON OF A BITCH!" she screamed. *"WHO THE* ***HELL*** *DO YOU THINK YOU ARE?"* She continued to rail against me for several minutes without let up. But I felt no need to defend myself. My experience in Tanya and Sherman's community informed me, irrefutably, that this diatribe belonged not to me, but to Cindy's husband.

To be sure, my own issues had overwhelmed my intention not to play the instigator at this event. But I had played it in a conscious, if emotionally charged way. In point of fact, I had accelerated the process just as Cindy had requested (confirming the old adage, "Be careful what you wish for; you just might *get* it!").

And as Peck had predicted, our conflagration seemed to work some catharsis for the entire group. For just as soon as Cindy's outrage had dissipated, we were quite done with the "Chaos" phase and moved directly into "Emptying."

The doorway was gently opened by Jan, who began describing her own marital dilemma. She was an FCE leader/facilitator (though not officiating at this event), whose husband was chronically depressed. Jan feared he was slipping away from her and that the two would not survive much longer as a couple.

But unlike the thrust and parry going on between Cindy and me, Jan's statement was vulnerable and non-accusatory. She was neither judging her husband nor masking her own distress. Nor was she looking to the group to solve her problem or, for that matter, even to respond. Indeed, it was the very unconditionality of Jan's sharing that was about to spark us into "Community."

One of the group's two leaders now asked permission to step out of his role as facilitator and address an issue of his own. Apropos of my point to Cindy (and earlier, to Peck), he described his frustration at being unable to *sustain* "Community," not just in his everyday life, but even at these FCE events. He felt he was falling short of his calling, failing himself and those he was supposed to be serving.

This confession triggered a profuse response from an unlikely source. There was a salesman in the group, whose earlier pitch for "team spirit" (when we were stuck in Pseudocommunity) had fallen rather flat. ("Our group needs a *name,*" he had gushed, "like 'the Peaches'. . . or 'the *Magnolias!*'")

But the salesman's new proffer was poignant and deft. He described his own routine, driving from town to town, persuading strangers to buy things they didn't want. He was starved for some honest to God communication. And so very grateful for the last 15 minutes of it!

At this, the facilitator burst into tears; but the salesman kept right on facilitating. "However short you may have fallen, you've done *me* a great service. I never knew straight talk like this was even possible."

The facilitator now began to wail in accompaniment. A duet, not an accompaniment; two souls expressing their common anguish. Experiencing the human dilemma, perhaps from different vantage points, but feeling it, *sharing* it. And allowing us all to share it, first through their eyes, then through our own.

As I drove to the airport for the flight home, I had an almost physical sense of openness, from my throat to my navel, as though my very guts were hanging out. For days after the event, I found it difficult to focus on the mundane activities of daily life. We had been warned of such a "reentry phenomenon," so I was more patient with myself than I might otherwise have been. In an effort to interpret my personal state, I put pen to paper, as follows:

1. "Building community," as Peck calls it, means opening up our respective heart chakras. That chakra seems to respond sympathetically when someone else's heart stirs in close proximity. If the opening is permitted to continue, the group process accelerates as our own sympathetic vibration now sets off the next person's vibratory network.

2. The risk of this opening is that it exposes us to pain we've been preferring not to feel. As the pupil of the eye constricts to protect us from too much or too sudden an onslaught of light, so the heart chakra constricts in the face of our emotional pain. That's the gist of our defense mechanisms. (Only in this case, it's the "darkness" that constricts and the "light" that dilates.)

3. Nevertheless, as a pupil fixed in the wide-open position would more likely blind us than enhance our vision, so the heart chakra must accommodate to ever-changing interpersonal conditions. The task is to attune ourselves, ever more finely, to the amount and quality of the available (interactive) light. And that is what we should mean when we speak of "setting appropriate boundaries."

26

Mutual Therapy

If the above attempts to explain the sensational experience, what, if anything, had we done together in Knoxville relationally? To begin with, Cindy and I would not have taken each other's bait had we not each touched a sensitive nerve within the other's emotional network. I will go so far as to suggest that Jan's subsequent sharing about her marital distress was closer to what was really on *our* minds, had either of us been prepared to acknowledge it. Instead, we projected our marital conflicts onto each other.

"Projection" is the tendency to overreact when someone else's situation or behavior threatens to remind us of our own unresolved conflict. It seems we cannot help but notice, in others, the faults or problems we've been avoiding in our own lives.

Now if Peck is right, this isn't a bad thing, at least in the group-process setting he calls "community-building." For it was the very force of Cindy's and my own projection (the "Chaos" phase) that seemed to clear the way for Jan to share her marital dilemma more forthrightly. And while a working therapist would have been criticized for getting so emotionally caught up in the exchange (countertransference), my unconstrained subjectivity didn't make the gauntlet I threw down to Cindy less timely (or therapeutic).

As discussed in Chapter 11, reacting emotionally to the patient's process is something the therapist is trained to guard against. But this very self-monitoring also helps guide him to the real issue. For by noticing when his own buttons are feeling pushed, the therapist is actually *intuiting* what is going on with the patient.

Now if, as Dr. Peck suggests in *The Road Less Traveled*, "any genuinely loving relationship is one of mutual psychotherapy," the management of countertransference is something we must all come to grips with. For it is inevitable, indeed *desirable* that we become emotionally engaged in our loved-one's process (in which we, unlike the therapist, have a personal and ongoing stake).

But "mutual therapy" is further complicated by the fact that the communication is a two-way street. Unlike the therapist, we are called not just to monitor our emotions but to voice them. And it is that very give-and-take that tends to bring us to the therapist (or the marriage counselor) in the first place. In short, it is much harder to *have* a relationship than to counsel one.

That said, objectivity and emotionality need not be at cross-purposes, much less mutually exclusive. What the conventional wisdom overlooks is that maintaining objectivity once the emotional dust has been kicked up is a spiritual, not just a clinical challenge. It is about keeping the *ego,* not the emotions in check.

Ego is the mother of all defense mechanisms. When a conflict erupts, it circles like a vulture, hoping to subvert the parties' will to communicate. And when ego penetrates our emotional field, defensiveness is the behavioral product. Defensiveness is our neurotic stasis, energized by projection, then commandeered by ego. It is emotion gone bad.

Our very reactivity to someone else's communication thus alerts us that objectivity is, to that extent, *at risk*. But the interaction may yet prove a blessing depending on what happens next. If we hand ego the reins, our relational work-in-process degenerates into defensiveness, sabotaging the communication. But if ego can be contained, emotion will *ripen*—into the same intuition on which the therapist ultimately relies.

In this sense, all emotion is nascent intuition. Intuition, in turn, is emotion, inuring itself to ego so as to attain its wisdom. And such wisdom—born of emotion, not intellect, lights the way to our eventual healing.

27

Addiction

I got a nice card from Cindy a week or so after the workshop. She wrote that she and her husband would soon be going off to spend three days at a cabin, on their favorite lake. "Now I know we have that time to reach community *together,*" she added.

My own catharsis from the Knoxville encounter had less to do with my marriage than with an issue Blumenthal and I had been exploring. He had pointed out an addictive quality to my pursuit of intensity in relationships, that I seemed to use interpersonal process to gain some temporary relief from my depression. (This was the primary conflict I had projected onto Cindy the moment she displayed her own addictive craving for community.) I thus found myself wondering, both during the weekend and afterwards, whether I had just fallen off the wagon.

One of the most eloquent speakers at the Knoxville FCE event was Keith Miller, author of *The Taste of New Wine* and other Christian spiritual books. Miller's very topic was addiction, and he noted that one could be addicted to intensity as well as to alcohol, drugs, food, sex or other sensations. He defined addiction as "any behavior that makes you feel better but isn't in your best interest . . . and which you cannot seem to *stop.*"

Was I then the one palming process off as intimacy? The thought of so perverting my hard won insight was sobering indeed. So I searched for a way to temper the addictive component of my own communicative zeal.

The answer I came up with was to monitor not the intensity of my interactions *per se,* but my motivation going into them. Was my agenda relational or sensational? (Did it involve a "who" or merely a "what"?) If it was sensation I was after, then I was using people, merely *pretending* to relate. But if my goal was truly to communicate, i.e., taking account of the other person's needs and interests, not just my own, then I needn't abstain from all ensuing interpersonal commotion.

And of course, the subtlety with which ego insinuates itself into even our most well-meaning interactions would have ruled out total abstinence, in all events.

28

Feelers and Thinkers

In the early, happy days of Tanya and Sherman's community, Mr. Dillon had a way of evening things up, so that whoever seemed to have come out on the short end of the processing stick would be given their due. He posed the question, "Whose gift was greater, Jesus' or Judas'?"

Dillon's point was that without Judas to betray him, Jesus could not have fulfilled his purpose. So once a consensus was reached as to who had played the "Jesus" and who the "Judas" of a particular transaction, the latter (assuming his energy had shifted) would be welcomed back into the communal fold like the prodigal son. Our pledge not to stigmatize each other was the ethical corollary of Tanya's assurance, during our first visit to the community, that "once the energy is resolved, it's as though the conflict never existed."

But we often fell short of that high moral mark, and I tended to serve on such occasions as the Pharisaic scapegoat. The collective judgment would be that I had mortgaged my faith to some well reasoned doubt; my love to a pride driven propriety.

Many "spiritual" people tend in this way to play the "heart" off against the "mind." Faith and love are credited to the former, while the latter gets the rap for worry, doubt and having to keep our agreements. When Gurudeva Ji once had the misfortune of being sued, he commented that the law was "pure mind" (a most disheartening pronouncement for us few lawyer-devotees).

Dillon also occasionally bad-mouthed the mind, and I bought into this when I preached to my brother Fred that "the heart has more to offer." If I were writing that letter today, I would say that heart and mind no more vie with each other than do liver and kidney.

We had a version of this false dichotomy operating within our own nuclear family. When the kids were small, we played a game in which I would try to steal their "spins." The closest translation for this would be their "smells"; but what I was after was the warm, fuzzy sensation of rubbing my face right up against theirs, just as they were awakening from a long night of "spinning."

But when our middle boy was about four, he started spurning me at these snuggling sessions, in favor of his mother. "What's so special about *her?*" I asked in a stern but playful tone. "She has love spins," came the reply. "Well what kind of spins do *I* have?" I demanded. *"Strong* spins," came the answer.

———— ———— ———— ————

If the FCE workshop in Tennessee was about husbands and wives, the one in Denver, two years later, was about parents and children. There was Alfred, a therapist, whose German father had been in the SS during World War II. No chip off the old block, Alfred was soft-spoken and conciliatory. Then there was Gene, who was bitter about his mother's parenting. "Her best just wasn't good enough," was Gene's angry mantra.

True to form, I again played the antagonist. For about half an hour, Alfred had been moderating our pseudocommunity, as if to fill a perceived leadership vacuum. When I finally called him on this, I sounded much more like his father, the Nazi, than I had intended. The group leapt to Alfred's defense, declaring that he was coming "from his heart"; whereas I was obviously quite stuck "in my mind."

Henry, a Rabbi with some standing in FCE circles, eventually spoke up for me. Remembering me from the Tennessee event, he served as a kind of character reference. Henry admitted that on first making my acquaintance, he too had felt threatened by my penchant for cutting to the interactive chase. Nevertheless, he now suggested it was the group that was stuck, in a picture of what "heart" was supposed to look like: permissive, not percussive; comforting, not confrontational.

Temperamentally, Henry is more the conciliator than the antagonist, making him *Alfred's* more natural ally in this debate. Indeed, his defection to my side of the heart-mind divide had a paradoxical effect on me. Far from reinforcing me on the argumentative merits, it put me in touch with a deep wound, a grief I had not previously been aware of.

It seems I had been waiting a long time for someone to see beyond my strength and acknowledge my heart. Unexpectedly, tearfully, I began sharing my hurt over having been misjudged, on many occasions, by people who had called themselves "spiritual" at my expense.

As if on cue, Louis, seated just to my right, lunged straight for my wannabe heart. With a dagger my ego had slipped him during a break, he denounced me to the group, as follows: "Elliot is so arrogant, he sent a letter to *Scott Peck*. He thinks he's on *Peck's* level!" Turning to me, Louis demanded to know how many books *I* had written.

But the tide had turned, and the group was now poised to make hamburger out of Louis for attacking me in my moment of "heart." Lucky for him, my own impulse (uncharacteristically) was to head off the massacre. It was suddenly self-evident that Louis (like Gene's mother) was doing the best he could. So I asked everyone just to lighten up and cut him some slack.

I think by this point, we were all running out of steam, so the session petered out rather anticlimactically. But I left it feeling done with my karma as the personification of unloved mind. And glad to have relinquished that unflattering role, in which I had so long felt typecast.

29

Relationship Building

Community-building with strangers, in a setting wholly removed from our normal relational contexts, can only accomplish so much. Despite the intensity (and sincerity) of our emotional outpourings, no piece of our ongoing life's work is present or at risk. Our families and bosses are not there to test the reality of the love we claim to be sharing.

Thus the dance we do at events like these should prepare us for something unattainable at the workshop itself. I would call the goal sustained relational intimacy. In this sense, the workshop provides a safe environment ("a safe place to be in terror," as one of our Denver FCE participants put it) in which to practice the art of *relationship*-building. But it is only when we get back to our families and jobs that the safety net is removed and the real fun/terror begins.

One of the things I was mulling on my return from Denver was the difference in my energy *vis-a-vis* Alfred and Louis. As noted above, my reproach to Alfred had been harsh, even by my usual, unsugarcoated standard. It seems that over the years, I had come to pride myself in the acuity with which I held other people's feet to the processing fire. But when Henry's vote of confidence put me in touch with what was driving the acuity, it yielded to a less forceful, more compassionate self-expression.

As I replay this progression in my mind's eye, I realize that appearances to the contrary notwithstanding, none of my interactive dramas has been any less unilateral a *tour de force*. Behind the merits of my every fervent pronouncement lurks this unanswered koan: Does *Elliot* (not his putative cause) finally have something he wishes to share? Is he ready, at long last, to be heard? (Or, as his fellow barristers might say, is he once again just "making his record"?)

The psychospiritual correlatives for this are:

Telling (Making the Record) → Sharing
Listening → Hearing
Facts/Information → Communication
Preaching/Teaching → Reaching

The left side of the arrow is more sensational than relational. And it is the relational quality of the right side that enlivens the interaction, transforming an intellectual or emotional exchange into a heartfelt communication.

I thought about the implications of the above for communication in my normal contexts and with Diane in particular. What was keeping me from seeing that my wife was also doing the best she could? If I could relate to her more right-sidedly, would her "listening" convert to "hearing" in response to my increased "sharing"? Was that not the Newtonian essence of the eternal soulmate theory, that a genuine shift in my energy would have to evoke some commensurate response in hers?

And what if the theory was just wrong? Suppose I made such a quantum individual leap only to disprove, once and for all, the relational hypothesis. Where would that leave my long-suffering marriage?

"Well, what have you got to lose?" the nymph of my in-dividual process reprised. "If you can pull it off (and live to share about it), will the relational impact any longer matter?"

PART FIVE

BETTING THE FARM

30

Jeffrey and Frieda

Most of our parents were suspicious of Tanya and Sherman, if not overtly hostile. But Jeffrey Shwartz didn't have a judgmental bone in his body. He even attended a trance circle and was quite moved by it. "You sure lucked out getting *that* one for a father in law," Sherman remarked to me afterwards.

Frieda Shwartz, on the other hand, put the following on a package she sent to us in Normal:

ATTENTION POSTMAN: MY DAUGHTER IS CAUGHT UP IN A CULT! PLEASE PLACE THIS ENVELOPE *DIRECTLY IN HER HAND*. (IF SOMEONE OFFERS TO ACCEPT IT FOR HER, **THEY ARE NOT TO BE TRUSTED!!!**)

This was classic Frieda. And in the face of her histrionics, Jeffrey was careful never to raise a dissenting peep.

When the Shwartzes went out to dinner, the first order of business would be for Frieda to demand a better booth. Once re-seated, Jeffrey would ask her what he was in the mood to eat. His passivity was the perfect complement to her bitter but more honest bite—like the sweet and sour she ordered for them when they ate Chinese.

I could write a cartoonish volume about my in-laws, had they not been, *together,* such brutal parents to my wife. When young Diane once froze up during a piano recital, Frieda berated her, right there in front of the audience. A few years later, an already fragile teenager was making out with her first boyfriend on the backyard swing. Through a bedroom window, Frieda branded her a whore and a slut.

Jeffrey's response to such atrocities was unfailingly gentle. "My poor *boobela,*" he would say, with great but useless empathy.

I don't air these dirty linens to get back at anyone. The fact is, the events I'll soon be recounting would be incomprehensible without the backdrop they provide.

When we were in our late thirties, Frieda announced she had a serious family matter to discuss (in light of which she asked me to step out of the room). The bombshell was that Jeffrey had been married before, and Diane had an older half-sister! Little Lori was only six when her mother sent Jeffrey packing. And he never looked back.

But now, almost half a century later, Jeffrey's first *boobela* was flying to Chicago for a reunion with her father. It was of course the daughter (not Jeffrey) who had initiated the reunion. And Frieda, not Jeffrey, who was finally spilling these beans (to "prepare" Diane for the meeting with her unheard of half-sister).

The neurotic irony of this goes back at least another generation. When Jeffrey was a teenager, his own father had walked out on the family. Leaving footsteps his son would follow a decade later, it was Myron Shwartz who first made his way from Brooklyn to the Windy City. Where he and Jeffrey would eventually live our their estrangement, just a stone's throw from each other.

For Jeffrey never braved another meeting with his father. Near the end of Myron's life, he asked to see his son again, but was rebuffed. This may have been the only time Jeffrey ever said "no" to anyone. Maybe it was his sense of loyalty to his mother, back in Brooklyn. (Just the mention of Mama Clara's name always brought a giant lump to Jeffrey's throat.)

Such striking disparity between the parents, one playing the evil perpetrator, the other, a noble victim, is apparently quite common. As described earlier, my own family of origin had a similar charade going on. But I believe the self-deception was even greater in the Shwartz household. Diane grew up idolizing her dad, installing him on the very pedestal he'd erected for Grandma Clara.

We had long recognized the pattern of domination and submissiveness in the Shwartzes' relationship, and that we had acted it out, to a lesser degree, in our own marriage. But as much hard work as we had done over the years, this revelation about Jeffrey's former life was our first real clue to an aspect of Diane's pathology that had eluded us (along with Tanya and Sherman, two psychoanalysts and several marriage counselors). Like her father and grandfather before her, my wife was capable of jettisoning what appeared to be close, familial relationships . . . without missing an empathic beat.

31

Diane

Early in her professional training, Diane was interviewing the mother of a new patient on the children's psychiatric ward. The woman was relating an incident in which her young son had pinched her. Suddenly, as if there were no other way to convey the information, she leaned forward, took hold of the fleshy part of Diane's arm and gave *her* a prolonged and painful pinch.

Diane was so nonplussed, she pretended nothing untoward had happened. Her supervisors, observing through a one-way mirror, later asked why she hadn't responded to the assault (even to the extent of saying *"ouch"*). She could give them no real answer.

I suspect it was because young Diane's interactive life was no less carefully scripted than young Elliot's. We had both taught ourselves to repress our interpersonal discomfort, so as not to have to deal with it. But while I *looked* like someone out of touch with his feelings, Diane's warm affect and psychological *savoir faire* portrayed a young woman very much in touch with hers.

Husbands and wives can learn a lot by observing how their spouse performs for his or her own parents. I remember being struck by the immediacy with which Diane would go into a kind of soft-shoe routine for her mother. It was an animated medley of pleasing, positive expressions and behaviors, calculated to keep the enemy distracted and at bay.

The "idea" of this defensive banter was to display total confidence and control, thereby preempting any possible criticism by Frieda. Like the scrambling device the cable stations use to make their signal unintelligible, Diane filled the airwaves between her mother and herself with a million bursts of positive chatter, effectively blocking the signal in both directions.

I don't blame her for this. The signal her mother was emitting was so critical and controlling, the only alternative to deflecting it in this way would have been to confront it head on. But Diane and her father had long renounced any such direct, confrontational approach in favor of an underground resistance. Their tactic was to display a cheerful obedience in the presence of the enemy's overwhelming firepower . . . while engaging in a lifelong guerilla campaign.

Unfortunately, we human beings lack the flexibility of the cable companies to scramble our communicative signals on a selective basis. We don't easily lower and reassemble our defenses to suit the diverse energies of all the people we encounter. Nor, in interactions with our most significant others, can we screen out their harmful spectra and let their remaining light pour in. We may be more nimble with those who've not gotten so far under our skin. But try growing up in Mrs. Shwartz's house and telling *her* about appropriate boundaries.

This habit of obliging chatter and behavioral niceness severely limited Diane's ability to establish a strong relational bond with anyone. For example, she had an aunt

(Frieda's own half-sister) who was a regular visitor to the Shwartz household all the years Diane was growing up. Aunt Edna had a daughter Diane's age, and the two girls were frequent playmates. Their common grandmother, Grandma Susie, lived with the Shwartzes, so Edna and her daughter were always present at family gatherings and holiday celebrations.

But shortly after Grandma Susie died, Frieda told Edna she never wanted to see her *or* her daughter again! And as far as I know, she never did.

Some years later, I asked Diane if she had any idea how Aunt Edna was doing. "No," she responded with only token interest. "Well," I suggested, "do you think maybe we should stop by and say hello? After all, Edna hasn't seen our fifth-grader since he was a toddler, and I'll bet she would welcome the visit." "Good idea," Diane concurred; "let's do that."

We had a pleasant enough visit, but it struck me that as willingly as Diane had gone along with my suggestion, she'd never have seen (or perhaps even thought of) her aunt again had I not proposed visiting her. How, I wondered, could Frieda have so thoroughly (and *vicariously*) purged my wife of all emotional ties to her aunt and cousin?

Much of Diane's individual therapy over the years had focused on her tendency to be, like her father, passive and compliant. She did dabble with some "assertiveness training" when it came into vogue in the late '70s and early '80s, but without any lasting effect on her anemic sense of personal authority. When we moved to Tanya and Sherman's community, our relational tendency to have things my way suddenly came under intense scrutiny. For a long while, my strong spins were closely monitored, lest they even *think* of putting the muscle on Diane's love spins.

Within a few years after leaving the community, however, our marriage had reestablished its previous homeostasis. This was most obvious in relation to the disciplining of the children. Long after our boys were capable of contributing around the house, Diane continued to perform most of the household chores single-handedly. Between her housekeeping, shopping, cooking, chauffeuring and part-time practice, she managed to keep herself frantically busy, while the kids spent hours each day in front of the TV.

I would come home from the office to encounter my wife's palpable but never more than simmering frustration. And in an osmotic process the mechanics of which still baffle me, I'd soon find "my own" anger at the children rising. Within a short time, I would hear myself hollering at them for not being more helpful to their mother.

Diane's response to these remonstrations was invariably protective toward the kids and critical of my "harshness." The boys would then storm off to their rooms, angry at me. When they came back out, their mother would comfort them, and for the rest of the evening, I'd be the odd man out.

One day, I decided to try a different approach. I called a family meeting to see if we couldn't all pitch in and make Mom's life a little easier. We agreed the kids would be responsible for setting and clearing the table and we'd each take a night doing the dishes. Diane expressed enthusiasm for the new plan and thanked me for initiating it.

But within a few days, a peculiar thing started happening. Diane would finish eating before the rest of us and begin clearing away the dishes. Her stake in the familial status quo was that extreme (and that unconscious). What she wanted, it seemed, was not to resolve her frustration but to continue channeling it *through me.*

Perhaps this was how she vented a lifetime of pent-up rage. Or how we transmitted to the next generation the legacy of our own childhood experience. On Diane's side of the family tree, I played the overbearing Frieda; she, the kindly but ineffectual Jeffrey. And on my side, I brought trouble home from work with me each night, just as my father had done a generation before.

It seems odd that after all these years, something as benign as the clearing away of the dinner dishes now shined a spotlight on this multi-generational pathology. But in the months that followed, I became hypersensitive to the family dynamic this small incident had revealed. It was, for me, a kind of wake up call.

My relationship with the boys began improving in direct proportion to my abstention from their process with their mother. I simply stopped reacting, at least overtly, to Diane's ever-simmering frustration. She, however, took this withdrawal as some implicit criticism of her (which in a sense, it was). She accused me of never being satisfied with her "the way she was." And our debate over who was really judging her (and for what) created just enough friction to keep the home fires burning. A controlled burn, in lieu of the larger conflagration just over the next hill.

So here we were, down at last to the core of our defensive symbiosis. Our clinical trial of the eternal soulmate hypothesis was reaching its logical conclusion. If the theory held water, my resignation as Frieda's stand-in should create a neurotic vacuum . . . in which Diane/Jeffrey could no longer remain invisible.

32

Smoking Jeffrey Out

What would have happened if, 40 years ago, Jeffrey Shwartz had decided to be a different kind of person. Suppose he had awakened one day and told Frieda he would no longer tolerate her mistreatment of Diane (and himself). It's impossible to predict the outcome of such a confrontation, and no one can know for sure that any of the lives involved would have turned out better or happier. But a generation later, I was determined to put it all on the line. I refused to serve any longer as Diane's emotional mouthpiece.

My sessions with Blumenthal were increasingly taken up with accounts of Diane's passive-aggressive behaviors, so much so that he thought she should be back in treatment. Diane, as always, was amenable; so my psychiatrist suggested she go see Dr. Schechter.

I don't know whether Blumenthal had any such thing in mind, but Dr. Schechter embarked immediately on a psychoanalytic course, seeing Diane three times a week. And for a while, the treatment seemed to be going well. I remember her pausing, mid-sentence, to remark that a cliche she'd just uttered was one not heard in years . . . one her *mother* had often used. Another time, while looking in the mirror, she was struck by the fact she had her mother's exact skin coloring. It seemed propitious that she was finally beginning to identify with the oppressor-parent, rather than the one who had played the victim.

I should have kept that observation to myself. Diane passed it on to Dr. Schechter, who became irate. Where did this lawyer/husband, himself the number one oppressor-suspect, come off making psychoanalytic interpretations?

So I was once again a meddler in someone else's "work" with my wife. But I was not about to replay the drama of 20 years earlier. I declined Diane's invitation to vie with another analyst for the stewardship of her psyche; and did my best to respect a boundary she herself refused to recognize.

Then she started smoking marijuana. This had been a sore spot between us over the years, and resuming the habit at this juncture was her way of saying, "Put *this* in your pipe and smoke it." Of course, had she been capable of just coming out and saying (or doing) that, she'd have looked more like Frieda than Jeffrey. Her real agenda wasn't to get high, but to get "caught."

I came home one day to find one of my old pipes lying on our back lawn, with marijuana residue in the bowl. Diane had called me earlier, at the office, to say she was going for a hike at Black Hawk Arboretum. So I had an hour to think about how or whether to respond to this new provocation.

My plan was not to take the bait. But I found myself incapable of interacting casually with her that evening, as if nothing were going on. So I asked, as matter-of-factly as I could, "What's the deal with the marijuana in the back-yard?"

Diane expressed total perplexity, denying any knowledge of the matter. It was as if to suggest some burglar, having settled for just my old pipe, then tarried in the yard to get high. Newly mellowed and repenting of the theft, he left the pipe right there—and probably a nice note (carried off by the wind), thanking us for our hospitality (and apologizing for any inconvenience).

After reflecting on the unlikelihood of the above, I said, in a quiet but impassioned voice, "So help me God, I'll not be your policeman or your prosecutor again, no matter what you do. I can't pretend I didn't find this marijuana, or that I'm comfortable with you smoking it. But I can and do recognize that it's not for me to decide whether you should or shouldn't be getting stoned. In fact, I'm open to the possibility that's something you may just need to be doing right now."

Diane looked me square in the eye and said, "I don't care whether you approve or *disapprove;* I have *not* been smoking marijuana. And I've no idea how that pipe got into the backyard!"

I teetered for a moment. She seemed anything *but* stoned. Indeed, this was the very self-assertiveness I'd been agitating for. Could I be so invested (subconsciously) in keeping her on the defensive that I was jumping to one more logical but erroneous conclusion? "Well, do you think one of our *boys* is into marijuana?" I asked, before making my apology. "I don't know," Diane soberly responded.

I called the boys into the kitchen, where we were having this discussion. I showed them the pipe and told them the ashes in the bowl smelled like marijuana. I asked if they knew anything about this, or how the pipe had gotten into the backyard. Now it was my 10 and 11-year-old sons' turns to deny all knowledge of the pipe and its contents.

I was utterly stumped. But then, in a decisive departure from how I had dealt with such impasses in the past, I truly did take control. Addressing myself to the boys, I announced my verdict:

Well here's the deal. I found this marijuana in the backyard. I believe Mom was smoking it, as she has in the past from time to time. That's not the end of the world. In fact, some people think alcohol is worse for you than marijuana.

You've probably also heard me tell Mother I sometimes feel more like her parent than her husband. I think what's going on here is, by arranging for me to find this marijuana, she has just set me up to continue relating to her in that familiar but unhealthy way. Well, I've just told her, and I also want to tell you, it's not my job (*or yours*) to keep Mom from smoking marijuana.

Now let's go watch some TV.

33

For the Love of the Children

The above interaction was a significant event for me, my wife and my boys. For perhaps the first time, I had held my own with "Jeffrey," without morphing into "Frieda."

Within a minute or two, Diane came into the TV room, where the boys and I were now seated. She told them she had indeed been smoking marijuana and apologized to us all for having lied about it. Then she left the room.

When I mentioned this incident to Sarah, she called it a major breakthrough in our relationship. I would now characterize it as a giant upping of the ante, for both of us. Our relational homeostasis had been dealt a severe, possibly a mortal blow. I suggested earlier that what defense mechanisms are to the individual, the relational status quo is to the couple. That meant we would now be finding out whether there was anything besides our neurotic symbiosis holding us together. Whether we were or were not "eternal soulmates."

I also learned from this experience that our children were the Achilles heel of Diane's neurotic complex. As adaptive as her neurosis had proved in the face of all the psychological, spiritual, individual, conjoint, conventional and quackish therapies we had tried, what had worked, at least

for the moment, was a direct but clean response to her manipulative behavior *in the presence of the children.* Did that
mean she loved them but not me—that she would choose
them over her neurosis as she was supposed to have chosen
her eternal soulmate?

This certainly wasn't the first apology the boys had gotten from their mother. In dozens of family meetings over
the years, neither of our shortcomings had been white-
washed. But Diane's foibles had always been passive, the
kind of nonfeasance of which Grandpa Shwartz had so often been guilty; some regrettable omission or disappoint-
ing lack of follow through.

The real shift in the collective energy of our family was
that Diane could no longer be Jeffrey without Frieda there
to help her pull it off. And for the first time, she had shown
herself capable of some Frieda-like *mal*feasance. The kids
had seen her haul off and *do* something "bad," something
in which no one else was the slightest bit implicated.

So the jig was up. Dad and the boys were suddenly bask-
ing in each other's company, love spins and strong spins
commingling as though made for each other. And Mom,
though uncharacteristically the odd parent out, was at last
fully present and accounted for.

She was off in her room, but energetically, she had finally showed up. She was nobody's victim. And no one was
loving her any the less.

34

In Sickness and In Health

What did we really mean when we said, "for better or for worse, in sickness and in health"? If my wife of 25 years had become wheelchair bound, say as the result of some degenerative illness, would anyone feel I was justified in divorcing her to avoid the anguish and hardship associated therewith? Would it be different if she instead suffered an emotional malady that deprived me of sustainable adult companionship?

Ever since our days with Tanya and Sherman, I'd been committed to the eternal soulmate vision of marriage as an arena for personal growth, fertilized by relational conflict and spurred on by the desire to preserve and enhance the relationship. Implicit in this paradigm was the assumption that love truly could conquer all, including neurosis.

This had become for me an article of faith. In spite of the disillusioning outcome of our involvement with Tanya and Sherman's community, I still believed each increment of individual growth brought with it, by definition, a greater capacity to love. And that the concomitant of one spouse's increased love was a decreased capacity on the part of the other to continue inflicting pain. Almost as though the latter, when all was said and done, would have no real choice but to grow.

I had also assumed that the effect of each positive energy shift within the relationship was the reestablishment of the homeostasis on a higher level; that our combined neurotic toxicity was diminishing in the process, like an infection responding to a course of antibiotics.

But suppose this latest assault on my wife's defenses, however well-intentioned, was setting the stage for a desperate counter-offensive. What if her pathology, far from becoming less virulent, was only conserving its force for an apocalyptic last stand in defense of the neurotic fatherland? Or mutating, with each new dose of tough love I administered, into some finally impervious, love-resistant superbug.

Whatever the uncertainties, taking this theory of psychospiritual growth and relationship to its limit seemed the natural progression of everything our life together had been about. We would soon find out, "for better or for worse," whether the extreme measures we had taken to resuscitate our marriage in the early '80s (i.e., moving to Tanya and Sherman's community) had earned us anything more than another decade or so on marital death row.

"What a nice young man I met today," Diane mentioned casually over dinner. "You know, the one who stands at 44th and Stevens with the 'Will Work for Food' sign." Of course I knew the guy she meant. Her bleeding heart made him a virtual toll booth for us at the intersection.

"Well, he was in the *7-Eleven,* getting a drink, and we struck up a conversation. His name is Mitch. It turns out he's all alone here, cut off from his family on the East Coast. The poor kid has a really good heart, in spite of a terrible family history."

Diane quickly found herself engaged in social work of the more traditional kind, networking with various agencies in Mitch's behalf. Within a few weeks, he'd been to the house and met our boys, our dog, our cat and our fish.

The next escalation came during a busy, pre-holiday afternoon. Diane called me at the office to ask a favor. "Mitch has been getting increasingly depressed and has nowhere to go for Thanksgiving," she said. "I'd really like to invite him to spend the weekend with us."

I flashed on a scene from several years before. On our living room couch, Frieda had sat curiously clutching her purse. She was explaining how she and Jeffrey had first gotten together. Like Mitch, Jeffrey had no money and no friends or family in the state. Frieda had given him her phone number at a party, and a few days later, he called her up . . . from jail! (He had let some tickets go unpaid, and the police had picked him up on a bench warrant.)

Now, in the suspenseful manner of a well-crafted closing argument, Frieda shifted slightly in her seat, thus redirecting our attention to the purse still perched precariously on her lap. Reminiscent of the sealed envelope in the O.J. trial, we wondered how its contents would be woven into her theory of the case. Finally, she reached in and retrieved her smoking gun.

It was the tattered receipt for the bail bond she had posted to get her derelict future husband out of jail! I'm not making this up. For 45 years, it had served as her license to dominate, proof positive she had no alternative but to lead Jeffrey around by the nose.

It seemed all too pat, but could my wife now be creating, in Mitch, someone who was more "Jeffrey" than *she* was?

Someone in relation to whom she might experience the competence and authority her mother had so monopolized? (And was she also saying, "You want me to be more like *Frieda?* As you said to Cindy at the FCE event, 'be careful what you wish for . . . .'")

"I don't like what I'm seeing," Sarah said a few weeks later, with real concern in her voice. As mentioned above, Sarah had been entirely positive about my handling of the marijuana incident. But her uncharacteristic pessimism, as soon as Mitch came into the equation, had an unlikely effect on me. I became almost smug. For some reason, when it came to this impending business with Mitch, I felt peculiarly out of harm's way.

There's tremendous irony in this. When we joined Tanya and Sherman's community, I looked back with embarrassment on the naivete with which I had ignored all energetic warning signs leading up to my wife's prior infidelity. I was the man who said, "Sure, dance with my wife; just don't touch my car."

But this time, I was hardly oblivious to what was unfolding before my very eyes. This was not denial on my part, but a deliberate bracketing of my emotional response. I was determined to relinquish all control over Diane. If the choice was now between surrendering to her neurosis (by retaking the reins) or letting it do its worst, my course was set.

"Sure," I heard myself say. "Invite Mitch to join us for Thanksgiving . . . if you think it's the right thing to do."

35

For Better or for Worse

Day by day, I watched Diane blossom. The presence and initiative she was suddenly exhibiting, albeit in relation to another man, was a wonder to behold. Machiavellian as my clinical detachment may seem, my wife was emerging as if from a long sleep. Not just behaving (or misbehaving), but *interacting,* as a self-possessed, autonomous human being.

And really *caring* about someone. I do not for a moment believe her attraction to Mitch was fundamentally perverse. What is our passion but compassion, spiked by the neurotic stimulus of our subconscious agenda? I was not about to suppress this awakening in Diane, mixed bag though it might prove to be, in order to preserve a marital status quo that had outlived its usefulness.

"Thanks for the heads-up," I told Sarah, confident that if the time came for me to inject myself into my wife's budding relationship with Mitch, I'd know when and how to do so.

I was wrong about that. I did not know. And neither did Sarah. Diane began stoking my suspicion, seducing Mitch and me simultaneously. Phone messages that were less and less discreet. Unexplained absences. What should "not taking the bait" look like in this situation?

I finally confronted her. "It doesn't matter to me whether you are or aren't having an affair with this guy," I lied. "Your willingness to push that button again, to play the affair card, is betrayal enough. It's over between us."

Sarah actually suggested I hire a private detective. How odd that sounded coming from her. Like NASA, with its network of spy satellites, proposing an old fashioned, 50-cent mousetrap. "You miss the point, Sarah," I chided her. "If I have to entertain such an idea after all Diane and I have been through, the damage is done. What would photographs do for me, one way or the other?"

A month later, Diane made a suicide gesture. She walked into the living room, where my eldest son and I were sitting, and held her arms out wide, like Jesus on the cross. They were smeared with blood. When she then started running back toward the bathroom, my son had to help me wrestle her to the floor.

But only then did the real illness show itself. With no physical room to maneuver, Diane simply snapped herself back into performance. "It's all right," she said soothingly to our 19-year-old, like an outsider doing crisis intervention on someone else. "Let me go back in the bathroom and clean myself up. This was stupid."

"LOOK AT THIS!" I shouted to our son. *"This,* not those scratches on her arms, is the sickness. Do you see what just happened—what she did to us *just then?"*

"I'm sorry, my son," I continued, almost weeping. "Maybe I've drawn you into this situation because I needed someone else to *see* it. Not the suicide gesture; the *unreality.* I don't think I can bear this much longer, and I'm going to need you and your brothers to understand."

It was a Sunday morning, but it seemed appropriate to call Dr. Schechter. "Do you think she's dangerous?" he asked, for the first time soliciting my input. "Extremely," I wanted to say, "but not in the physical sense you have in mind."

After hearing my take on the incident, Schechter asked me to bring Diane to his office. On the way there, I told her that at the end of her session, I wanted a word with her and her psychiatrist. "That's fine *with me,*" she so typically obliged.

Precisely 45 minutes after she had closed it behind her, the door to Schechter's inner sanctum swung back open. "What can I *do* for you?" he inquired, as he might have of the Fuller Brush man. I repeated the phrase to myself and counted to ten.

"I'm not sure," I replied. "But this morning's drama reminds me what an incredible actress my wife can be. So I'm now wondering if she's even shared with you the havoc we've been enduring as a family. Were you aware, for instance, that . . . "

"I can't say whether Diane's been having an affair," Dr. Schechter smugly preempted me.

"And that *so* isn't the issue," I seethed.

"I *can* give you a referral for marriage counseling if you want one," he persisted.

"Are *you* nuts?" I wanted to scream.

"Here's what I'd be interested in," I continued, straining to remain civil. "Blumenthal has just retired, and I'm going to need someone to help keep my own head screwed on straight. I'd like that to be someone with whom you're on speaking terms, someone you have confidence in. Would it then be possible, without violating any professional strictures, for the *two* of you to confer? Or even for all four of us, perhaps, *to talk?*"

"That kind of thing has been done," Dr. Schechter conceded. "I suggest you go see Dr. Blakey. I did my own analysis with him, and there's no one in whom I have more confidence. In fact, I'll call and ask him to get you in right away."

36

The Psychiatrist's Psychiatrist

I had some wonderful sessions with Dr. Blakey, who quickly understood the implications of Diane's pathology. And how it now had a gun to *all* our heads (including Dr. Schechter's).

"There are two things I really need your help with," I said to him. "First, I have to know, once and for all, what's the matter with my wife. "I don't know why it's important. I'm not sure it will change anything at this point. But if she were experiencing physical symptoms as alarming as what we've been living through, I'd sure as hell be demanding a diagnosis."

That request seemed eminently reasonable to my new psychiatrist.

"The second thing I'm wondering is, what am *I* still up to in all this?" I gave him the background of our experience in the community, my own family history, my work with Dr. Blumenthal, the guru, Mr. Dillon, everything. I also told him about Diane's home life as a child and her previous and current treatment, from my vantage point. Then I described the events leading up to the current crisis.

"Your grasp of the dynamics at play here is laser-like," he complimented me. "Well here's what's scaring the *shit* out of me then," I shot back—"and all the more so after hearing that from you! What happens next if this process is allowed to play itself out?"

"That's a serious worry," he answered. "Her next step could be suicide, or some other dangerous drama."

"Well should I give it up then?" I asked. "Are we better off separating?"

"I'd like to meet Diane before speaking to that," he stated, rising from his chair to signal the end of our session.

"Great," I practically shouted, feeling hopeful for the first time in a long while. "How do we arrange it?"

"Let me talk to Dr. Schechter," he replied.

"And about that second issue," I pressed on at the risk of encroaching on the next patient's time. "Does the fact that I'm still *with* Diane attest to my love for her . . . or to the perniciousness of my own pathology?"

"Another fair question," Blakey acknowledged. But the therapeutic hourglass had dropped its final grain of sand.

BOOK TWO

37

What's Past Is Prologue

According to Einstein, insanity is "doing the same thing over and over again and expecting a different result." Had there been time in that session with Blakey to address the $64,000 question ("What was *I* still up to in all this?"), I might have pressed the case that any further thought of salvaging this relationship, however "laser-like," should surely call my own sanity into question.

But events intervened before we could have that conversation. As recorded in the Prologue, "The phone rang, and it was Mitch . . . ." So as they wheeled Diane into surgery, I pondered the more immediate and finally irreducible question: Did I want any longer to *be* the one by Diane's side?

The Sunday paper had "Peanuts" on the front cover. It was fall, and Lucy was once again asking Charlie Brown to run up and kick the football. "Sure, and what happens if you pull the ball away?" Charlie Brown demanded. "You could always *sue,*" Lucy answered. "She's right," Charlie Brown muttered, preparing for one more process with his eternal soulmate. "If she pulls the ball away again, I'll sue."

Dr. Blakey did eventually have a session with Diane, after which he offered up the following diagnosis: "Neurotic (*severe*); but not psychotic. She has what we used to call an 'as-if' personality disorder. This diagnosis isn't in the DSM,[14] but it was widely used some years back. It denotes an individual who lives her life 'as if' someone else's thoughts and feelings are her own. Looking at it from a systems perspective, you've had an 'as-if' family."

I flashed on a note I'd received just a few months earlier. Diane and our eldest son had sung with me at a Holocaust Memorial Service, after which a congregant had written: "Our sincere thanks to you and your family for a moving rendition that enriched this year's *Yom Hashoah*. We survivors are especially emotional about families. And to see *yours*, harmonizing so sweetly, was touching."

Dr. Blakey confirmed that Diane's pathology went back at least two generations. "You've finally corrected the systemic part of the illness. The trick now will be to manage the system so that it is minimally disrupted while she works through this on an individual basis. Off the record," he added, "and knowing what I know about the two of you, I wouldn't rush to divorce her."

Sarah seemed of a different persuasion. She counseled that if I chose to stay with Diane, I should be prepared to accept her "the way she is." But Sarah also held out the prospect of "a more suitable partner, waiting in the wings."

"I'm not done with this marriage," I told Sarah, apparently making my decision for the present. "At this late stage, I can't just cut my losses, call it a 'good lesson' and start from scratch with someone else. In the eyes of all who thought they knew us, Diane has gone from 'saint,' to 'harlot,' to 'mental case.' As far as I'm concerned, she's the

---

[14] Diagnostic and Statistical Manual, published by the American Psychiatric Association.

same person she's always been. So if I loved her before, why would I stop loving her now that her neurosis has finally seen the light of day? Especially when *I'm* the one who has insisted on 'outing' her."

"As for accepting her 'the way she is,' I'm not sure I understand the implications of that. I'm prepared to give up trying to force my wife to 'grow.' But I'll never go back to the pretend marriage we've had. There will be no more holding ourselves out, not to our children or anyone else, as anything but the broken relationship we truly are."

"From here forward, the picture will match the reality. If we can pull that off, I believe we can both stay out of further harm's way."

38

Dominion

But I soon reconsidered. I can still see the stricken look on our 12-year-old's face when I told him I had to move out. Just two months ahead of our 25th anniversary, I took an apartment . . . and filed for divorce.

The central allegation in a divorce petition is that the marriage is "irretrievably broken." To my left brain, the affair with Mitch made that open and shut. Yet I still couldn't say to myself (or to our children) that I no longer "loved" their mother, at least as I was then still wrestling with the term. And with that other term . . . "irretrievably."

The kids didn't like coming over to the apartment. There wasn't much for them to do there, and our "outings" together felt contrived. So before long, I was just "hanging" with them a few hours at a time—at "their house." Soon, their mother started saying, "Well, you're already here; you might as well just stay for dinner," which only seemed to make sense. (And by now, of course, Mitch was totally out of the picture.)

As a result of the divorce filing, we had a financial arrangement in place. But between uninsured hospital bills (from the suicide attempt), divorce lawyers and my apartment rent, money was getting tight, to the point that even my left brain was now open to creative thinking.

So when my 6-month apartment lease was up, I refashioned the divorce petition into one for legal separation; under the terms of which I would move back "home," but into a separate bedroom on my own end of the house—and as Diane's *tenant*.

We also went in for a few joint sessions with Dr. Blakey around this time. At one of those, he introduced us to a concept he called "dominion."

Blakey began by describing how hard it had been for him, early on in his career, learning to deal with suicidal patients. "What I finally realized," he said, "was that you have to be willing to walk right up to the abyss with the patient. But in the end, you also have to be willing to let him or her jump off."

"The gift of the therapist in this situation is his willingness to be there, for better or for worse, when the moment of truth finally comes. This allows the patient to find out if he really wants to live or die. But it also ends the therapist's vulnerability to blackmail. And you, Elliot, have walked that walk with Diane."

Then he told us the story of "Sir Gawain and the Hag." Sir Gawain was unsuccessful in love, so he went to the Hag and asked her "what a woman truly wants." She promised to tell him . . . but only if he first agreed to *marry her!* Then magically, the Hag transformed herself into the most beautiful woman Sir Gawain had ever seen.

Falling instantly in love, Sir Gawain proposed to her on the spot. "There's one catch," said the Hag-turned-Princess. "I can be a hag in public and a princess for you, in private; *or vice versa*. But if you still want to marry me, *you* get to decide in which setting I'll bewitch." And to give reality to the decision now before him, she began flashing back and forth, from Hag to Princess, and Princess to Hag.

"I love you, my darling," said the smitten Sir Gawain. "And I give that choice right back to you."

At once, the Hag turned beautiful again, even more beautiful than before. And *stopped flickering*.

"You have liberated us *both,*" she exclaimed. "By giving me my *dominion*—by loving both the Princess *and* the Hag, you have broken the evil spell that kept me cycling back and forth between the two.

"And to answer your question," she continued . . . "what a woman truly wants . . . is to *have* her dominion."

39

Satsang at Synagogue

The *Shema Yisrael* prayer, the watchword of our faith,[15] is followed in the prayer book by three paragraphs, taken from the Books of Deuteronomy and Numbers. The first begins, "Thou shalt love the Lord thy God with all thy heart, with all thy soul and with all thy might." The third commands us to wear fringed garments (commemorated by the prayer shawls worn at synagogue).

But it's that middle paragraph that gives our Rabbi fits. It reads:

> *And it shall come to pass, if ye harken diligently unto My Commandments, that I will give the rain of your land in its season, that thou mayest gather in thy corn and thy wine and thine oil. I will give grass in the fields for thy cattle, and thou shalt eat and be satisfied. But take heed, lest your heart be deceived and ye turn aside and serve other gods and worship them; and the displeasure of the Lord be aroused against you and He shut up the heaven, so there shall*

[15] *"Shema Yisrael, Adonai Eloheynu, Adonai Echad* -- Hear O' Israel, the Lord Our God, the Lord is One."

be no rain,[16] *and the ground shall not yield her fruit;*
and ye perish quickly from all the good land which
the Lord giveth you.

One Saturday morning, in the midst of all the tumult
described in the preceding chapters, the Rabbi was giving a
d'var Torah (discourse) on the above. "I have a hard time
accepting that good behavior brings prosperity or that God
withholds His bounty from sinners," he confessed, adding
that both were contrary to his own life experience. He even
admitted feeling *patronized* by this scripture—then opened
it up for comments from the congregation.

From my seat on the opposite side of the dais, I eventually joined the discussion. "God certainly rewards the good
and punishes the bad," I ventured. "It's the *application* that
is getting us in trouble. What *is* 'good behavior,' and what
is 'evil'? What fate represents God's reward? And what His
punishment?"

I then shared a story I had heard years before, at *Satsang.* A king had a servant who was an incorrigible opti-
mist. When anything remotely negative occurred, he would
immediately pipe up, "Whatever happens is good!" This
got a bit tiresome, but the king put up with it.

Then one day, as the servant was giving the king a
shave, his hand slipped, drawing blood. "Shit!" the king
cried out. "Whatever happens is *good,"* the servant reflex-
ively retorted. *"Guards!"* the king commanded. "Throw
this insolent fool in the dungeon."

[16] At this writing, a severe drought in Israel has led the Chief Rabbi
to issue a call for fasting and repentance.

After staunching the bleeding, the king finished dressing, mounted his best steed and rode off into the forest, to hunt. There, a pagan band suddenly emerged from a thicket, surrounding him. "Our god demands a sacrifice," said the pagan chieftan. "What better prize could we have stumbled upon than the king himself?!"

They tied the king to a tree and began gathering wood for a fire. Then they noticed the cut on his face. "This man has a blemish," the leader intoned. "It is forbidden to offer him as a sacrifice." So the king was released unharmed.

Upon returning to the castle, a chastened king recalled his servant from the dungeon. "My profound apologies," he humbled himself. "That scratch on my face was indeed a blessing in disguise. I'll never punish you again for saying, 'Whatever happens is good.'"

But as the servant bowed and prepared to take his leave, the king had a face saving afterthought: "I can hardly deny that your slip of the blade turned out perfectly well *for me*," he again acknowledged. "But I trust your brief stay in that reeking dungeon of mine made it anything *but* good . . . *for you!*"

"On the contrary, Sire," the servant replied with unrepentant good cheer. Had you not, in your wisdom, dispatched me to the dungeon, I'd have been right at your side on that hunt. . . . And *I,* Majesty, . . . would have *had* no blemish."

40

An Energetic Scene Change

An important corollary of "whatever happens is good" is that there are no heroes and no villains in the story of my marriage. But it became clearer as the months wore on that I did not love Diane "as princess *and* as hag"; or, as Sarah had put it, "just the way she was." Instead, it seems I had been trying, over all these years, to transform her into my own vision of what a princess ought to be.

We surely cannot have been "eternal soulmates." For having wrung the last drop of emotional drama out of the relationship, there was no further energetic change . . . in it or in us. We had completed our karma together.

———   ———   ———   ———

The events described below followed close on the heels of everything related above. But I've waited another decade to write these closing chapters. I guess I wanted to make sure my new life was "for real."

I have also frankly feared being judged . . . for the jarring shift the saga (and my mood) are about to take. I know this is a head-snapping reversal of tone and fortune. But it was, after all, a very long time coming.

41

The Little Girl Waiting in the Wings

I was in third grade the first time I fell in love. A little girl I'd never seen before was walking by my house, on her way to school. On TV the night before, Cary Grant had showed me how to engage such an attractive stranger. "Hello beautiful," I called down to her from my front porch.

Without breaking her little-girlish stride, she gave me a smile (or was it a smirk?) and continued on her purposeful way. As it turned out, she and her family had moved in on Mellon Street, just five houses up from ours. In no time, I was hovering around whenever she came outside to play. Today, I believe they would call it stalking.

When the kid who sat in front of me at Rogers School pulled a diamond ring out of his Cracker Jacks, I knew I had to have it. He sold it to me for a nickel (which was a lot of money for a third-grader in those days). But without further modeling by Cary Grant, I was at a loss for how to present such a gift to a young lady. So I waited nervously in her driveway, clutching the already bent token of my affection. When she finally came out, I *threw* it at her . . . and ran straight home.

I remember this as if it were yesterday. And the words, a few weeks later, that broke my childish heart. She said she didn't like me hanging around her house every day, much less following her to her girlfriend's house on Beatty Street. Then, with a crushing giggle, she added, "I'd give you back your ring . . . but I've *lost* it."

With that, she turned and walked away, but not entirely out of my life. I kept an amorous if discreet eye on her as we progressed through elementary and high school, in our separate circles; before tucking away, for the next thirty years, the keepsake across which she wrote:

> Wow, the experiences we had could really fill a book, huh?! Wait, I remember you did give me a ring in 4th grade. How romantic! What memories. I truly wish the best for you.
>
> Love, Carole

So when Sarah mentioned a lovely lady waiting in my wings, Carole Berkowitz had been off my radar for three decades. But six months later, a flier arrived, announcing the 30th reunion of Peabody High School's Class of 1965.

And on the list of classmates who had already responded, Carole's name lit up like neon. Along with her marital status . . . *"divorced."*

After assuring me that the lovely lady was Jewish, Sarah had described her, rather cryptically, as "adventuresome but not aggressively so." Well, so far, so good. Carole's most salient trait, as I remembered her, was her perkiness. She was a social butterfly.

But what a disappointment that reunion turned out to be. She spent most of it catching up with the star of the basketball team, with whom she had gone steady all through high school. And my few minutes with her were more Pee Wee Herman than Cary Grant. "Weren't you on the debate team?" she politely inquired. And that was that.

But a year later, I was elected to the Board of the American Inns of Court, a national legal society. Their October meeting was in Washington, D.C., where I now knew Carole had been living for years. So, with nothing to lose, I called and asked her if she'd like to join me at the gala dinner dance the Board was hosting . . . at the U.S. Supreme Court. And she promptly answered, "Yes."

I still sucked at basketball, but over the decades, my stock as a debater had apparently gone up.

42

Full Court Press

The *modus vivendi* between Diane and me had now been in place for over a year. And it was *working,* in the sense that no new dramas were being instigated or enacted by either of us. We were cordial. We lived in the same house, co-parenting the kids. But our lives were otherwise separate and our own—as they had always been, only now without any pretense of intimacy.

Still, a psychic connection between us must have remained. For though I'd mentioned nothing to Diane about my impending date with Carole, the very first thing out of her mouth on my return from Washington was, "I have a feeling you're about to drop a bombshell on me." She had dreamed, that very weekend, that I was living "happily ever after . . . with a pretty new wife."

It is here I fear the reader's judgment that in some cavalier energy, suddenly footloose and fancy-free, I am about to trivialize the sturm and drang of our 25-years together (or worse, to lay it all at Diane's feet). But I cannot deny that when she shared that premonition with me, I was unmoved and unrepentant. I felt like Atlas, after stalwart eons of refusing to shrug, now giddy at the prospect of a liberating tickle from the woman in the wings. As far as I was concerned, Sarah's prediction (and now Diane's) of my happy future in a new relationship was a virtual *fait accomplis*.

In that conviction, I was certainly ten (or maybe a hundred) steps ahead of Carole. But a funny thing had happened at the end of that first date in Washington. Walking ahead of me to the hotel elevator, she did a sudden 180 and *kissed* me, rather passionately—the very thing I was hoping for back in her driveway, all those years before.

A few weeks later, she sent me this greeting card:

And this, more adult-oriented photo:

"I need a female perspective," I said to my secretary. "Is this the kind of picture a woman sends a man in whom she has no romantic interest?" "I don't *think* so," she correctly answered.

After that, our phone calls and correspondence became more regular and intense. I sent her a plastic ring, like the one from Rogers School. Then in November, I jumped on a plane and flew back to Washington, unannounced.

When I called her from my hotel, she told me this was neither appropriate nor feasible. In fact, she already had plans for the weekend—*with another man.* "You and I have only had a single date!" she reminded me.

It appeared that I was stalking her again. So I told her where I was staying and left it up to her whether or not to make further contact.

On one hand, my gambit proved more Cary than Pee Wee. She did show up at the hotel, and we talked for what was left of the weekend. But this conversation was not all sweetness and light. Carole made it quite clear that *her* dominion was not negotiable. While she was drawn to my self-confidence and initiative, she had a real aversion to being hemmed in—much less steamrollered.

I made it just as clear that I could not wait long in her wings if other men were taking center stage. Obviously, she needed to decide whether she wanted a romantic relationship with me, long-distance or otherwise. But we did at least begin discussing the kind of long-*term* relationship we both were looking for.

I also confessed it was a recent, gloomy comment she had made—about the very difficulty of long-distance relationships (and something about an upcoming, local *singles* event she was thinking of attending)—that had launched me so precipitously back to D.C. "If I'm moving rather quickly," I added, "at least I signaled my intentions with that impassioned poem I sent you the other day."

Only as I re-read that poem now do I grasp the irony . . . that in flying off to Washington, I had disregarded the very message of its second half:

To the Woman Waiting in My Wings

As our words grow into poems
and our notes become a song,
as the trees give way to forests,
so a true love comes along.

For a lover stokes our fancy
while the teacher feeds our mind.
Friend rides with us on the freeway,
sharing each mile at its time.

(And the therapist's a toll road—
never ours, however kind.)

But lover *and* teacher?
Counselor **and** friend?

If such a poem could be written,
it would surely be called "Husband";
such a song, heard first but faintly,
yet might "Wife" be in the end.

BUT GETTING *THIS*
IS MORE IMPORTANT
THAN GETTING *HER:*

You have earned you perseverance,
whereas patience is a flow.
Having honed your stern appearance,
you must learn to let it go.

To invite, but not to summons,
to allow, but not to beg.
Neither passion nor compassion
will give you the upper leg.

For the choice is *hers,* not yours, not God's,
to enter from the wings.
Otherwise, this breeze might just reprise
a script already screened. [17]

That weekend was the first of many rich, if sometimes fraught conversations. About the difference between a courtship and a seduction, having fun and playing games; between dominion and *carte blanche.* And that exquisitely fine line between standing one's own ground . . . and attempting to take control.

[17] It wasn't 24 hours after Fed-Exing the above to Carole that I proceeded—"oh what the *hell*"—to Fed-Ex her *myself.*

43

Meeting Half-Way

I had several days of depositions scheduled for New York City in mid December. So I e-mailed Carole a message I hoped she'd find proactive but not preemptive; romantic but not a rampage:

THE PLAZA ~ NEW YORK

SUN., 12/15 ~ WED., 12/18

TICKET TUES., VIA FED-EX

UP TO YOU (NO EXPECTATIONS)

FASTEN YOUR SEATBELT

Once again she showed up. Only this time, it *was* all sweetness and light.

Two weeks later, I was back in Washington for New Year's Eve. On the dance floor after a few cosmos, she pulled back, stared up at me seductively and purred, "Will you *marry* me?"

"Not tonight Dear," Cary coolly replied.

When I filled Dr. Blakey in on these developments (and particularly, when I linked them back to Sarah's prediction about the lady waiting in the wings), his feedback was sobering: "Of course you *realize* this is fantasy . . . *don't you?* I'm concerned you may be setting yourself up here, big time."

"Well, it certainly does *feel* fantastic," was all I was willing to concede.

44

Going for Broke

Certainly Blakey had a point, with which Carole was all too quick to agree. She began casting herself as a timely therapeutic intervention—just the romantic impetus that would finally extricate me from my long-moribund marriage (and living arrangement).

"That's a role I am willing to play for you," she said. "But after 25 years with Diane, you need to be on your own for a while. So think of me as just a pleasant intermezzo."

"I love it when you talk adult to me," I countered—then sent her back her greeting card, appropriately doctored:

My hope was to accelerate, not rationalize our romantic momentum, until it reached a critical mass that would bring Carole to me permanently, in Chicago. By now there was no curbing the passion pouring almost daily from my pen:

January 6, 1997

Dearest Carole,

Thank you for pointing out my naivete in thinking I might actually want to spend the rest of my life with you (instead of just driving up the stock of United Airlines). I trust you will allow me now my starry-eyed if not lawyer-like rebuttal.

My alternative to the leap of faith you so sensibly resist is what you yourself have called "trusting the process." It is neither childish nor reckless to envision ourselves opportunely positioned in (and under) *God's two* wings. From where, at the time of *our* choosing, we may confidently stride, not leap, to meet each other half-way (at center stage).

Then with only butterflies in our stomachs, we'll begin, at long last, to write our own script. And if we stay true to that script, i.e., honest with ourselves and each other, our past dramas will only nourish us going forward, like good compost. (Think hot sex blossoming into mature love-making.)

Carole, my darling, don't buy into the angst that dismisses this courtship as impetuous or unrealistic. It is the crowning achievement of my responsible late-blooming, the very hallmark of my growth. Take your own time to accept or reject my proposal; I respect your deliberation. For I know as well as anyone the price of a bad match.

But I also see the miracle of having lived to tell *each other* about it. So I'll run the risk of further pain for the chance to build a lasting happiness with you. I'm not suggesting we throw caution to the wind; only that we let the breeze of life flow through our circumspection to refresh and renew us.

There is always the risk that what we choose today may in the end be called another mistake. But every good thing begins in some unrealistic ether. The challenge is not to purge ourselves of fantasy but to help it take on flesh; to embody its optimism in a sustainable way.

I pray our hard won experience will thus improve, not stifle our prospects; that our sobering pasts will inform, not abort our future together. For my life does feel pregnant . . . with happiness.

So *MARRY ME, Carole Berkowitz*. Let me take you, after all these years, for granted. Then I'll make love to you with both the youthful ardor of my seductive fantasy and the staying power of your adult good sense.

And then maybe I can also get back to making us an honest living.

I love you.

ET

45

~~Making~~ *LETTING It Happen*

"Your letter took my breath away," she cooed in our next conversation. She also acknowledged that her caution carried a risk of its own. "'Good merchandise doesn't sit long on the shelf,' my mother taught me. I still don't think *you* should be rushing into a new relationship. But if I don't take advantage of your vulnerable state, someone else may come along and snatch you right out from under me."

We began tackling the logistics of starting a life together. Her older daughter, a senior in high school, would be off to college in the fall. But the younger girl, Amy, would just be starting high school. So I scrambled, once again with some help from my brother and sister, to put together the down payment for a house. (And made sure it was within the boundaries of the high school my own boys would soon be attending.)

It turned out that the son of one of my law partners was captain of the football team there, and his cheerleader girlfriend was just a year ahead of Amy. So when she came to Chicago with her mother a few months later, they were nice enough to show her around town. (Amy even got to shadow her new girlfriend at the school for a day.)

I settled into the new house, looking forward to a July

move-in date for Carole and Amy. But a few weeks later, just as everything seemed to be falling into place, Carole's Ex suggested Amy remain in Washington, *with him*. And she surprised Carole by taking him up on the offer.

"What kind of a mother would even *consider* moving away from her daughter at such a critical time in her life?" Carole now asked herself (and me). This was a crushing blow that threatened to scuttle everything.

So what do modern Jews do when faced with such a dilemma? They find a good psychiatrist. As it turned out, Carole had been attending a therapy group in Washington, so I flew in for yet another counseling session—with my *other*-woman and *her* therapist! I must say, it felt rather like a job interview. But I did come away with his psychiatric *"hechsher"* (seal of approval).

Indeed, Carole's therapy group was surprised at just how supportive of her move to Chicago he turned out to be. "Edward said that I should go to you," she later reported. "He was so definite about it that the group actually pounced on him. One guy said, 'I've never heard of a therapist being so directive.'"

"His only question to me was, 'Do you *love* him?' And my whole body answered, 'YES!'"

As for Amy, we held out hope that after a few months, she might reconsider her decision to remain in Washington with her father. If not, Carole was still working on a masters degree at American University, which meant she'd be flying back there one weekend each month for the next year and a half. So at least Amy (and her older sister) would get to see their mother on that regular basis.

One of Carole's closest friends was appalled at this compromise. "A Jewish mother doesn't abandon her children!" she inveighed. But fortunately, her opinion was outweighed by an even more influential one. Carole's own Jewish mother felt Amy should have a vote, but not a veto.

"I always liked that boy," she threw in.

46

Fruition

Thirteen years have now passed since Carole moved to Chicago, the best years of my life. We married just a few months after she arrived. (And four years later, Amy also moved here, to attend college.)

Those first years were certainly not without their challenges. We each had to recalibrate our marital expectations (and behaviors) in the face of partners very different than the ones we'd known before. And Carole had to deal with the recriminations of living so far away from her daughters.

I, on the other hand, had to acclimate to a home life that was finally working. This probably sounds strange, but after all my passionate causes, interpersonal dramas and related adrenaline rushes, I found myself functioning with a *dis*passionate efficiency that was for me, a new sensation.

For example, on the very day of Carole's arrival, I journaled the following:

> Now that the hard logistical work and emotional buildup are done, I've had to remind myself over the last few days what a very big deal this is! Does that mean I've lost my passion, or finally regained some equilibrium? After all the years of highs and lows, I feel strangely devoid of drama. It's like sitting down

to savor a delicious meal, with a healthy appetite,
but no need nor inclination to gobble it down.

The other thing I had to get used to was not being "in charge" in the relationship. After Diane's relentless passivity, Carole was a *force majeure.* So it took some time for us to negotiate just who was running what and where our respective red lines were. One night she said to me, playfully, "I don't get away with *anything* in this marriage; you call me on all my stuff! What the hell have I gotten myself into?"

But she no less calls me on all my stuff. And her firm individuality has made this marriage a stew, not a melting pot; corned beef and cabbage on a hot plate, not cream and sugar dissolving in some swirling spiritual brew. A phrase from the binding of Isaac comes to mind: *"V'yelchu shneyhem yachdav* -- And the two of them *walked on* together."

In my zeal, I may have misconceived the ideal relationship as some kind of a blending, rather than a walking-on together. Perhaps I was reading *"V'yelchu shneyhem yachdav"* as an imperative: *"**Those** two **shall** go together, **as one**."* But Carole has showed me that the blessing and the love are in the walking-on together.

Passionately, but side by side. *"Bis a hundert svansig* -- May it please last til we're a hundred and twenty."

CLOSING HYMN

Marital Change-Agents

One cannot force another soul to change.
Relationship eschews all guaranties.
And tandem growth admits no settled range;
some partners will advance and some recede.

Still, it is not for ourselves we change,
but for the love of another;
someone we love the way they are . . .
but also dearly want to love us *back*.

(And in that active hoping lies the fun
of all that we ourselves may yet become.)

Self sufficiency is ego's cubic zirconium.
Its bright but worthless glitter obscures the earthly path
which, ever ours to fritter, portends an other-half.
(Whose dowry, our honest vulnerability,
is the only true safe harbor.)

Do not mistake this for codependency.
True love bodes choice, not confinement.
But self-actualization is a half-truth;
the flower does not blossom for itself.

So BE THOU the one for whom I might change,
and love me enough to flourish with me.
Then, call me "Husband," and I will call you "Wife."
Our love for each other makes our own change possible,
choice meaningful, and life worth living.

SUPPLEMENTAL READING

TWO *MIDRASHIM* (ALLEGORIES)

A *Midrash* On Sensation:
Adam and Eve's Daring Gambit

When the Search-Committee started looking for a new rabbi, a whiff of insurgency was already in the air. It was clear that the congregation wanted someone quite different from Rabbi Frumewitz. It wasn't just the younger families (who wanted someone their children could better relate to). His stern demeanor and strict, bordering-on-Orthodox adherence to *halacha* (Jewish law) had driven off many potential new members.

As recently as a decade ago, he was still fighting tooth and nail to keep women off the dais (much less women in prayer shawls). Non-Jewish spouses were virtually frozen out of their kids' bar or bat mitzvahs. And let's not even talk about his position on homosexuality. ("I won't ask, but please don't *kvel* [brag]" was his standard refrain.)

The United Synagogue, of which Temple *Ner Tamid* is an affiliate, had not yet grappled with the issue of gays in the rabbinate but had recently ordained its first handful of women rabbis. If change was what the Committee had in mind, replacing Frumewitz with a female rabbi might be just the thing to shake up this historic congregation. So Rabbi Miriam Avtzeluches was invited to interview for the job. And from the very get-go, she seemed hell-bent to ruffle feathers.

Her visit coincided with *Shabbat Bereyshit,* the Sabbath

on which we read the creation story from the Book of Genesis. Dressed modestly (except for sequined head cover and iridescent striped prayer shawl), she strode right over to Rabbi Frumewitz on the dais and gave him an in-your-face bear hug. Then, fast enough to send her prayer shawl gallantly streaming, she spun around to address the congregation:

"Good *Shabbos* my friends, it's very nice to be with you this morning, *Shabbat Bereyshit* no less—when we make a fresh start by reading again from the Book of Genesis. So *who knows* [turning to stare directly at Frumewitz], maybe it will prove a new beginning for *all* of us!"

As if this and her very presence as Guest-Rabbi had not sufficiently made the point, she continued to go out of her way to stir the feminist pot. I was there. And what I am about to give you is a *verbatim transcript* (don't *ask* me how I got it) of her remarks, introducing the weekly Torah portion:

———   ———   ———   ———

When God first envisioned a soul in a body, my friends, *sensation* was what came to Mind. Seeing, hearing, feeling, smelling, and tasting. And, yes [*winking* here, like Sarah Palin], maybe just a touch of good-old-fashioned feminine intuition. But basically, the plan was for a network of neuroreceptors, hardwired to know light from dark, hot from cold, not-enough from too-much. And this idea of consciousness ensconced in matter was a very big bang indeed. [She looks up from her notes here, just to see if we *got* it.]

What God did *not* foresee, however, was physicality's potential as a medium for *relation*. It was Adam, on the ground, who conceived of an interpersonal operating system for the sensory mainframe. He asked for and was granted a companion. (All right, what he had in *mind*, probably, was someone exactly like himself; but let's give him all the credit—soon enough, there were *two* human prototypes, enjoying the fruits of the Garden.)

Now, it takes one for sensation; two for relation. But there was evening and there was morning, and Eve seemed, well . . . redundant! You heard me right, my friends. For *guess what*—it wasn't 15 minutes before Adam's sight and touch had confirmed that like everything else the Lord had made, Eve too *"was good."* But alas, her physical attributes did little to assuage his *relational* malaise.

"There's no such *thing* as loneliness," the serpent chided Adam. "It's all in your oversized, *homo sapiens* head!" But Eve knew better. Indeed, in all creation, only she was in full possession of that quintessentially feminine instinct, even in physical paradise, to gird sensation with relation. "I feel it *too,"* she declared. "Something's definitely missing."

And Eve knew this, you see, without needing to eat from the Tree of Knowledge. She was clear from the outset she'd not come all this way for sensation alone. No, she was here to *interact;* to express, *in and through* the physical, her *extra*sensory, image-of-God Essence.

But unlike the human genome, *relation* could not manifest on a simple "Let-there-be" from the Creator. Adam and Eve, together, would have to *work* at this—to make their incipient *feelings* flesh; and *keep on* breathing life into them.

And as if that weren't challenge enough for two babes in the woods, their relational agenda was beset, from the beginning, with a paradox. Eden's very abundance, you see, made it functionally obsolescent the moment relation was thought of. For the essence of relation is the will to share. But in the Garden, Adam and Eve already *had* everything; and only God (not each other) to thank.

So *that,* my friends, is why Adam—with Eve's encouragement, of course, had to give up his easy life and go out and find a good, steady job. He wanted, you should pardon the expression, to "bring home the bacon." So he could *share* it . . . with his *beshert* (beloved).

A *Midrash* On Relation:
"So Long Rabbi Avtzeluches"

Can you believe that even after the above fiasco, the insurgents mustered enough votes to invite that Rabbi Avtzeluches back? (Thank goodness it would prove to be her swan song.) And even after being advised she needed to come across a tad less creative (and a whole lot more scholarly/rabbinic), *this* is what she comes up with for the do-over:

———————   ———————   ———————   ———————

Shabbat shalom, my friends, it's wonderful and an honor to have been called back to visit with you again. This week's Torah reading contains a familiar but enigmatic verse, from Exodus 31:17, *"Uvayom hash'vii shavat vayinafash* -- On the seventh day, God ceased His work and rested." Now interestingly, this text expands upon the more concise account given in Genesis 2:2, *"Vayishbot bayom hash'vii* -- He *rested* on the seventh day." *"Shavat,"* in the Exodus formula, and *"vayishbot,"* in Genesis, are the same verb (from which, of course, the word *"Shabbat"* or "Sabbath" also derives).

But the additional verb in today's passage, *"vayinafash,"* adds a new and significant dimension. It comes from the root *"nefesh,"* which we usually translate, "soul." And according to a little known *midrash,* the verb *"vayinafash"* can be either transitive or intransitive: "intransitive" implying that at that instant, the Divine Essence "ensouled" or individuated *Itself;* or "transitive," meaning that on the seventh day, God imbued our already independent *physical* selves with an exemplar copy of His Own Divine Essence.

Now here is the important point, my friends: Either way, transitive or intransitive, the addition of the verb *vayinafash* turns a passive, sabbatical moment, one of cessation and replenishment, into an active, seminal one; a creative encore if you will—kind of like the one *I'm* having here today!

[She looks up hopefully, but we are not laughing. So she gives up on levity and manages, for a while at least, to sound half-way intelligent.]

For God does not just *rest* from His labors on *Shabbat,* you see; He becomes, *pari passu,* both the Subject and the Object, the Energy *and* the Mass of His own handiwork. In short my dear friends, God passes the creative torch over to us! (Or even more transitively speaking, we pick it up and *run* with it.)

I'm not suggesting here that God bows out of the creative process altogether on the seventh day. For as we say in our morning prayer, *"Uv'tuvo m'chadeysh b'chol yom tamid maaseh b'reyshit --* In His goodness, He renews daily His *physical* creation."* (And as we also recite on our joyous occasions, *"shehecheyanu v'kimanu --* He both fashions and *sustains* us" in our physical parameters.)

But I'm going to ask you now to think of this physical world God creates and sustains (including our own physical bodies) as but the backdrop for a second wave of creativity—Part Two in His/Her/Our ongoing evolutionary process. Picture the whole magnificent package, "the heavens above and the earth below, the world and all that dwell therein," as but a spiritual staging ground, a *tabula rasa* if you will. On which the most generative element, the very stem cell for all our future growth is—and this may surprise you, my friends . . . our physical (individual) *self-interest!* The very thing we bit into (or bit *off*) when Adam and Eve ate from the Tree of Knowledge.

[By now, more than a few of us are nodding off, so she may be worried this is going over our heads.]

Stay with me here, please, I know this is getting a bit complicated. In the cosmology I'm asking you to entertain, Adam and Eve turn God's orderly physical creation into their own *tohu vavohu* (primordial soup)—a world of material shortage and economic need; from which raw material they will now be charged with renewing daily the work of . . . *relational* creation!

For in the Garden of Eden, you see, we were like all the other animals—the top dogs perhaps; but from a spiritual point of view, still just half-baked. It was only outside Eden's safe and comfortable confines, at the synapse between the physical/sensational and the economic/interpersonal/*relational,* that human life as we know it could truly begin.

And it's at this point, I must give you fair warning, that the *midrash* and indeed my own theology are about to take a truly radical turn. For if you've followed what I've said so far, what some call "original sin" now becomes, *a fortiori,* the very *fruit* of Adam and Eve's ineluctable thrust for relation. *THEIR STEPPING UP,* not their falling down! And yet, my dear friends, this important, indeed courageous evolutionary breakthrough *does not sit well in heaven!* (And here, you see, is the biblical rub—*and the **real** falling down:*)

*"So you want a **RELATIONSHIP**,"* booms the Lord of Genesis to Eve. "Well suffer the pain of childbirth—then you'll have something to *relate* to your husband (and all those little ones) about! And you, Adam, will have to clothe and feed them. You may rue the day Eve convinced you there was more to life than frequent, unprotected and truly shameless sex!"

[Much awkward stirring, but now she definitely has our attention!]

"You say you ate of the forbidden fruit in order to be *like God?* The truth is, you want to *surpass* God. For I, the Lord, **AM ONE**. Now good luck to *both* of you."

If this sounds disrespectful, my dear friends, I beg your forgiveness. But since you are evaluating me as your potential spiritual leader, I owe you at the very least some honest self-disclosure. For I believe a rabbi's job, male or female, is to claim and speak her truth!

Well the God I worship is the Master/Mistress of all— the physical/sensational *and* what I'm calling the interpersonal/relational. And from that broader perspective, you see, the petty, jealous and vindictive god in today's Torah portion **[audible groans here, and from the balcony, one shrill *"WHAT DID SHE SAY?"*]** . . . is a creator who has lost his way! I must tell you, in short, that if you do call me to this pulpit as your Rabbi, *I will no longer be capitalizing **that** one's g!*

[With this, the Sextant, Mr. Perlmutter, starts ominously toward the dais, but Rabbi Frumowitz, from his newly upholstered Emeritus-seat, waives him off. As the ruckus continues to swell, Avtzeluches stares out at us, seeming flustered. Then finally, raising her arms and leaning into the microphone, she capitulates.]

O.K., *sha,* I didn't mean to antagonize you. We're all still Jews here, so you don't have to *agree* with me. But my friends (or should I now say, my *"detractors"*), it looks to me as if, in the course of subjectivizing the very objects of his creation, god's own objectivity has abandoned him. Maybe just the thought, the *aspiration* to such indigenous, *intervivos* effect—to the shared risk that is the hallmark, the *sine qua non,* of Adam and Eve's bold relational vision—proved too slippery a slope; down which his singular essence just could not transition.

But by now, you see, Adam and Eve's relationship was simply too far along to abort. So, constricting himself, god storms off in a huff . . . and has been laying down the law from a safe distance, ever since. *"VAYINAFASH!"*

[Despite the flourish, she pauses here as if out of steam. Maybe it has just sunk in that her employment at this synagogue definitely *has* been aborted! As she rummages distractedly through the remainder of her notes, the President consults with the Chair of the Ritual Committee: "Should we cut off her mic.?" he asks.

But Rabbi Frumowitz, the last one from whom you would have expected forbearance at this point, leans in and says, "All right, just let her finish. I must say, she's not entirely ineloquent; at least she knows her Hebrew." "And her Latin and her French," the President now thoughtfully concurs.

Rabbi Avtzeluches pauses further for a slow sip of water—a pregnant pause, it turns out. For her *worst is yet to come:*]

Whatever the explanation, my friends, since that ugly scene in the Garden, the lord of scripture has never been quite the same. Indeed, as we see in today's portion, it isn't long before he—let me just call him "little god" for present purposes . . . **[so many loud gasps here, she has to shout out the rest of this sentence]** . . . *repents of his solitude and asks the Children of Israel FOR THEIR HAND IN CHOSEN-PEOPLEHOOD.*

[Whereupon, stunned (uncertain whether she has just flattered us or added insult to the blasphemy), we emit an eerily unison, *"Huh??"*]

Yes, but even as his Higher Self is now courting us, at Sinai, with the Ten Commandments, *little-god* is attaching to them a congenital string: In the event of disobedience, he vows TO *VISIT THE INIQUITY OF THE PARENTS UPON THE CHILDREN*. And by that pronouncement, ladies and gentlemen, *psychology* is born!

[An alien silence settles in. We are puzzled, genuinely confused by this reference to psychology (a respected field in this congregation). What could she *mean* by it? Clearly savoring the moment, Avtzeluches takes yet another slow sip of water before enlightening us.]

Psychology, you see, is the very *impact* of our ensuing misbehavior unto the third and fourth generations. We thus become the instruments of little god's impassioned discipline, inflicting his collective punishment on each other. And to our great shame . . . and *this,* my friends (not our *genitalia*), is the real source of that shame . . . *on our own kinderlach* (offspring)!

[From the balcony again, "I *hope* I didn't hear the word I *think* I just heard."]

Our therapists call this "displacement." We displace (i.e., *dump*) onto our significant others every grievance we have ever suffered (or imagined) at the hands of Mom and Dad. In that way, we continue to act out our unresolved vertical (intergenerational) conflicts horizontally (within our own marriages).

Soon enough, our children get sucked into the pernicious process, initially as mere props for the drama now going on between their Mom and Dad. Until somewhere in their adolescence, they begin to parlay that horizontal *tsimmes* (commotion) into their own set of vertical grievances . . . against *us*. Etc. and boring etc., *l'dor vador* -- from generation to *farblondzhet* (befuddled) generation.

[Several people are now walking out, but the ushers are doing nothing to stop them.]

It took one for sensation, two for relation; and three or four such stiff-necked generations to enmesh ourselves in the neurotic conundrum. The upshot, my friends, is that we now waste half our lives and money in therapy, trying to distinguish our actual, real-time issues from things that are old (or someone else's). And only by unraveling this great psychospiritual puzzle (which other traditions call *karma,* by the way) will we begin to free ourselves and our progeny from a covenant in sore need of renegotiating.

For we've been *backpedaling* since the day Adam and Eve called sensation into the service of latent relation. Our emotional exile is a vestige of little god's primordial hurt feelings. And it's high time we helped him (and each other) get *over* it!

Shabbat shalom.

About the Author

Elliot Talenfeld lives with his wife Carole, in Phoenix, AZ. Formerly a Clinical Professor at Loyola Law School (Los Angeles), then partner at a major Phoenix law firm, he also holds a Master of Counseling degree, is a National Certified Counselor (NCC) and serves as a cantor each fall, on the Jewish High Holidays.